# AND ALL SHALL BE WELL

Dedicated to the memory of

**TIMOTHY**

# *And All Shall Be Well*

an anthology of poems
to give comfort

## Herbert W. Wood

ISIS
LARGE PRINT

Oxford, England
Santa Barbara, California

Published in Large Print 1989 by Clio Press,
55 St. Thomas' Street, Oxford OX1 1JG



British Library Cataloguing in Publication Data

And all shall be well: an anthology of poems to give comfort.
1. Poetry in English — Anthologies
I. Wood, Herbert W.
821'.008

ISBN 1-85089-385-3

Printed and bound by Robert Hartnolls Ltd.,
Bodmin Cornwall

Cover designed by CGS Studios, Cheltenham

# CONTENTS

"Give sorrow words; the grief that does not speak
Whispers the o'erfraught heart, and bids it break."

*William Shakespeare*
**Macbeth**


"Blessed are they that mourn: for they shall be
  comforted."

*Jesus Christ*
**St. Matthew's Gospel**

# FOREWORD

It gives me great pleasure to write the foreword to this book. In 1981 I first met Bert Wood and through discussion I learnt that he had lost his youngest son a little time before in a climbing accident on the Continent.

He showed me a sample of the poetry which he had written to help him to overcome his grief, and also went on to say that he found great help through reading poetry.

Now, eight years later, he has compiled this book of poetry and verse with the object of helping other people who are experiencing a similar tragedy. All the profits from the sale of this verse anthology are to go to CRUSE, the organization which provides Bereavement Care.

He has put this book together with care and great love of the written word, and I am sure that it will bring happiness to the people who read it — through extensive reading and research he has uncovered a wealth of poetry and verse.

*Geoffrey Barlow*
Sussex

# INTRODUCTION

I have sought in the midst of my own grief, during the dry after-time of mourning and the following desolate years, to draw together these tears and flowers — the verses of poets born of our own and other times, from our own English and other cultures.

An anthology on the subject of grief and death might promise to be depressing, especially to those already depressed, but the purpose of this collection is to offer solace and give comfort. So many of the poems in the first and second sections reflect the experiences of those who have lived or who are presently living with sorrow; the sense of loss so acutely expressed, the bitter-sweetness of past joys and sadnesses, of mundane everyday life re-called in subdued memories touch upon familiar chords within each one of us. Many poems are, in truth, love songs sung to a broken lute. We hear echoes from within the deep well of compassion reverberating to our own response.

The third and fourth sections predominantly proclaim a message of hope. We face the reality and inevitability of death and, whilst I have admitted a few poets who dwell upon the finality of mortal existence, most voices speak of belief in an other life beyond and of a loving God whose realm transcends and surpasses our life of transient happiness, fears and sorrows; whose presence takes us beyond the vale of tears into the light.

It has not been my intention to produce a definitive collection of poetry on this type of reflective verse. That would, indeed, have been a formidable task as all poets acquainted with sorrow have written of their anguish either from the depths of despair or, and frequently, in the subsequent mood of tranquil, ofttime melancholy, reflection. Every final parting stabs at the heart, leaving an irreplaceable absence. So much sorrow lingers on.

Some excellent anthologies already exist. The present selection seeks only to supplement these and concentrates exclusively on the verse form. I have endeavoured to let the individual voices of the poets speak for themselves, out of their own sufferings and revelations about the meaning of life and death.

I believe that the writers of the lines in these pages have shared something of their innermost thoughts and feelings, of their very lives, with me. Such sharing has been both a comfort and a privilege which I trust, dear reader, you may also experience in taking up this book.

I wish to express my deep gratitude to members of my family, the many friends and not least, to Veronica Babington Smith at Isis, who have given me so much encouragement. It is really due to them, through their suggestions, contributions and guidance, that this collection of verses has finally made its appearance.

*Bert Wood*

# PART ONE

# THE CLOAK OF SORROW

# 1. GOOD-BYE

The last of last words spoken is, Good-bye—
The last dismantled flower in the weed-grown hedge,
The last thin rumour of a feeble bell far ringing,
The last blind rat to spurn the mildewed rye.

A hardening darkness glasses the haunted eye,
Shines into nothing the watcher's burnt-out candle,
Wreathes into scentless nothing the wasting incense,
Faints in the outer silence the hunting-cry.

Love of its muted music breathes no sigh,
Thought in her ivory tower gropes in her spinning,
Toss on in vain the whispering trees of Eden,
Last of all last words spoken is, Good-bye.

*Walter de la Mare*


# 2.  THE CLOAK, THE BOAT, AND THE SHOES

"What do you make so fair and bright?"

"I make the cloak of Sorrow:
O lovely to see in all men's sight
Shall be the cloak of Sorrow,
In all men's sight."

"What do you build with sails for flight?"

"I build a boat for Sorrow:

O swift on the seas all day and night
Saileth the rover Sorrow,
All day and night."

"What do you weave with wool so white?"

"I weave the shoes of Sorrow:
Soundless shall be the footfall light
In all men's ears of Sorrow,
Sudden and light."

*W. B. Yeats*


## 3. REQUIEM

Pour out your light, O stars, and do not hold
Your loveliest shining from earth's outworn shell —
Pure and cold your radiance, pure and cold
My dead friend's face as well.

*Ivor Gurney*


## 4. A.G.A.

Sleep brings no joy to me,
Remembrance never dies;
My soul is given to misery
And lives in sighs.

Sleep brings no rest to me;
The shadows of the dead
My waking eyes may never see
Surround my bed.

Sleep brings no hope to me;
In soundest sleep they come,
And with their doleful imagery
Deepen the gloom.

Sleep brings no strength to me,
No power renewed to brave:
I only sail a wilder sea,
A darker wave.

Sleep brings no friend to me
To soothe and aid to bear;
They all gaze, oh, how scornfully,
And I despair.

Sleep brings no wish to knit
My harassed heart beneath:
My only wish is to forget
In the sleep of death.

*Emily Brontë*


## 5. GRIEF'S HARMONICS

At evening, when the lank and rigid trees,
To the mere forms of their sweet day-selves drying,

On heaven's blank leaf seem pressed and flattened;
Or rather, to my sombre thoughts replying,
Of plumes funereal the thin effigies;
That hour when all old dead things seem most dead,
And their death instant most and most undying,
That the flesh aches at them; there stirred in me
The babe of an unborn calamity,
Ere its due time to be delivered.
Dead sorrow and sorrow unborn so blent their pain,
That which more present was were hardly said,
But both more *now* than any Now can be.
My soul like sackcloth did her body rend,
And thus with Heaven contend:—
"Let pass the chalice of this coming dread,
Or that fore-drained O bid me not re-drain!"
So have I asked, who know my asking vain;
Woe against woe in antiphon set over,
That grief's soul transmigrates, and lives again,
And in new pang old pang's incarnatèd.

Francis Thompson


## 6. MY DEAREST JULIA

Oh! can or can I not live on,
Forgetting thee, my love forgone?
'Tis true, where joyful faces crowd
And merry tongues are ringing loud,
Or where some needful work unwrought
May call for all my care and thought,

Or where some landscape, bath'd in light,
May spread to fascinate my sight,
Thy form may melt awhile, as fade
Our shades within some welkin shade,
    And I awhile may then live on,
    Forgetting thee, my love forgone.

But then the thrilling thought comes on,
Of all thy love that's now forgone:
Thy daily toil to earn me wealth,
Thy grief to see me out of health,
Thy yearning readiness to share
The burden of my toil and care,
And all the blessings thou hast wrought
In my behalf by deed and thought.
And then I seem to hear thee calling,
Gloomy fac'd with tear drops falling,
    'Canst thou then so soon live on,
    Forgetful of my love forgone?"

William Barnes

## 7. HOLY SONNET  XVII

Since she whom I lov'd hath payd her last debt
To Nature, and to hers, and my good is dead,
And her Soule early into heaven ravished,
Wholly on heavenly things my mind is sett.
Here the admyring her my mind did whett
To seeke thee God; so streames do shew their head;
But though I have found thee, and thou my thirst
has fed,

A holy thirsty dropsy melts mee yett.
But why should I begg more Love, when as thou
Dost wooe my soule for hers; offring all thine:
And dost not only feare least I allow
My Love to Saints and Angels things divine,
But in thy tender jealosy dost doubt
Least the World, Fleshe, yea Devill putt thee out.

John Donne

## 8.  WINTER GRIEF

Life so brief…
   Yet I am old
     with an era of grief.

The earth unveils
   a sad nakedness
And her hills
   droop round my sorrow.
Into the stillness
   living things scream
and only the nerveless dead
   get tranquillity.
From the funereal mould
late asters blaspheme.

Herbert Read

## 9. THE SEPARATIONS OF GRIEF

Tenderness  and the blessed tension of water
are elsewhere adept. Water's secularity
is a tap, a toothless mouth sleep;
can rim vacancy, or torn laughter;
will pour its welfare upon the downright hands
of gratitude. Waters of separation
are inseparable. And so is grief.

*Jon Silkin*

## 10. DECEMBER

"No, don't stop writing your grievous  poetry.
It will do you good, this work of your grief.
Keep writing until there is nothing left.
It will take time, and the years will go by."
Ours was a gentle generation, pacific,
In love with music, art, and restaurants,
And he with she, strolling among the canvases,
And she with him, at concerts, coats on their laps.
Almost all of us were shy when we were young.
No friend of ours  had ever been to war.
So many telephone numbers, remembered addresses;
So many things to remember.
The red sun hangs in a black tree, a moist
Exploded zero, bleeding into the trees
Praying from the earth upward, a psalm
In wood and light, in sky, earth and water.
These bars of birdsong come from another world;

They ring in the air like little doorbells.
They go by quickly, our best florescent selves
As good as summer and in love with being.
Reality, I remember you as her soft kiss
At morning. You were her presence beside me.
The red sun drips its molten dusk. Wet fires
Embrace the barren orchards, these gardens in
A city of cold slumbers. I am trapped in it.
It is December. The town is part of my mourning
And I, too, am part of whatever it grieves for
Whose tears are these, pooled on this cellophane?

Douglas Dunn

## 11. ABSENCE

When thou art absent,
Grief only is constant,
My heart pines within me
Like the sighing of reeds
Where water lies open
To the darkness of heaven,
Voiceless, forsaken.

The bird in the forest
Where silence endureth,
The flower in the hollow
With down-drooping head —
Ah, Psyche, thy image! —
My soul breathes its homage;
But cold is this token,

Cold, cold is thy token,
When from dream I awaken,
By sorrow bestead.

*Walter de la Mare*


## 12. *From* IN MEMORIAM

59.

O Sorrow, wilt thou live with me
 No casual mistress, but a wife,
 My bosom-friend and half of life;
As I confess it needs must be;

O Sorrow, wilt thou rule my blood,
 Be sometimes lovely like a bride,
 And put thy harsher moods aside,
If thou wilt have me wise and good.

My centred passion cannot move,
 Nor will it lessen from to-day;
 But I'll have leave at times to play
As with the creature of my love;

And set thee forth, for thou art mine,
 With so much hope for years to come,
 That, howsoe'er I know thee, some
Could hardly tell what name were thine.

*Alfred, Lord Tennyson*

# 13. *From* **AMBARVALIA**

My wind is turned to bitter north,
   That was so soft a south before;
My sky, that shone so sunny bright,
   With foggy gloom is clouded o'er:
My gay green leaves are yellow-black,
   Upon the dank autumnal floor;
For love, departed once, comes back
   No more again, no more.

A roofless ruin lies my home,
   For winds to blow and rains to pour;
One frosty night befell, and lo,
   I find my summer days are o'er:
The heart bereaved, of why and how
   Unknowing, knows that yet before
It had what e'en to Memory now
   Returns no more, no more

*Arthur Clough*


# 14. HOLY SONNET 1

Thou hast made me, And shall thy worke decay?
Repaire me now, for now mine end doth haste,
I runne to death, and death meets me as fast,
And all my pleasures are like yesterday;
I dare not move my dimme eyes any way,
Despaire behind, and death before doth cast

Such terrour, and my feeble flesh doth waste
By sinne in it, which it t'wards hell doth weigh;
Onely thou art above, and when towards thee
By thy leave I can looke, I rise againe;
But our old subtle foe so tempteth me,
That not one houre my selfe I can sustaine;
Thy Grace may wing me to prevent his art,
And thou like Adamant draw mine iron heart.

*John Donne*

## 15.  PSALM 142

1.   I cried unto the Lord with my
     voice; with my voice unto the Lord
     did I make my supplication.
2.   I poured out my complaint before
     him; I shewed before him my trouble.
3.   When my spirit was overwhelmed
     within me, then thou knewest my path.
     In the way wherein I walked have they
     privily laid a snare for me.
4.   I looked on *my* right hand, and
     beheld, but *there was* no man that
     would know me: refuge failed me; no
     man cared for my soul.
5.   I cried unto thee, O Lord: I said,
     Thou *art* my refuge *and* my portion in
     the land of the living.
6.   Attend unto my cry; for I am brought
     very low: deliver me from my

persecutors; for they are stronger
than I.
7.   Bring my soul out of prison, that
I may praise thy name: the righteous
shall compass me about; for thou
shalt deal bountifully with me.

*King David*

## 16.  ENVOY

Go, songs, for ended is our brief sweet play;
 Go, children of swift joy and tardy sorrow:
And some are sung, and that was yesterday,
 And some unsung, and that may be to-morrow.

Go forth; and if it be o'er stony way,
 Old joy can lend what newer grief must borrow:
And it was sweet, and that was yesterday,
 And sweet is sweet, though purchased with sorrow.

Go, songs, and come not back from your far way:
 And if men ask you why ye smile and sorrow,
Tell them ye grieve, for your hearts know To-day,
 Tell them ye smile, for your eyes know To-morrow.

*Francis Thompson*

## 17. ON ANOTHER'S SORROW

Can I see another's woe,
And not be in sorrow too?

Can I see another's grief,
And not seek for kind relief?

Can I see a failing tear,
And not feel my sorrow's share?
Can a father see his child
Weep, nor he with sorrow fill'd?

Can a mother sit and hear
An infant groan an infant fear?
No, no! never can it be!
Never, never can it be!

And can he who smiles on all
Hear the wren with sorrows small,
Hear the small bird's grief & care,
Hear the woes that infants bear,

And not sit beside the nest,
Pouring pity in their breast;
And not sit the cradle near,
Weeping tear on infant's tear;

And not sit both night & day,
Wiping all our tears away?
O, no! never can it be!
Never, never can it be!

He doth give his joy to all;
He becomes an infant small;
He becomes a man of woe;
He doth feel the sorrow too.

Think not thou canst sigh a sigh
And thy maker is not by;
Think not thou canst weep a tear
And thy maker is not near.

O! he gives to us his joy
That our grief he may destroy;
Till our grief is fled and gone
He doth sit by us and moan.

*William Blake*


## 18. PAIN

The cry of man's anguish went up to God,
"Lord, take away pain!
The shadow that darkens the world Thou hast made;
The close coiling chain
That strangles the heart: the burden that weighs
On the wings that would soar —
Lord, take away pain from the world Thou hast made
That it love Thee the more!"

Then answered the Lord to the cry of the world,
"Shall I take away pain,
And with it the power of the soul to endure,
Made strong by the strain?
Shall I take away pity that knits heart to heart,
And sacrifice high?

Will ye lose all your heroes that lift from the fire
White brows to the sky?
Shall I take away love that redeems with a price,
And smiles with its loss?
Can ye spare from your lives that would cling unto mine
The Christ on his cross?"

Indian prayer


## 19. HASTE ON, MY JOYS!

Haste on, my joys! your treasure lies
  In swift, unceasing flight.
O haste: for while your beauty flies
  I seize your full delight.
Lo! I have seen the scented flower,
  Whose tender stems I cull,
For her brief date and meted hour
  Appear more beautiful.

O youth, O strength, O most divine
  For that so short ye prove
Were but your rare gifts longer mine,
  Ye scarce would win my love.
Nay, life itself the heart would spurn,
  Did once the days restore
The days, that once enjoyed return,
  Return — ah ! nevermore.

Robert Bridges

# 20. A DREAM

Last night my mother died
Again, in a dull dream.
Some master I did not know
Had set me to strange work,
And then the message came.
O God my grief broke
From a lead-coffin-cloud
Of inward snow
In tears too cold to weep:
For when my dream began
I could have come to her
And standing beside her bed
Kissed her dear brow again.
She felt so much more dead
Dying thus in my sleep
And I not there.

*Patrick Dickinson*

# 21. ELEGY

She went so quietly from earth
As if I followed a bright stream
That suddenly slid into the ground
And still I heard the under-sound
    Like feelings in a dream;
The lark a channel of music making
Called her to flow uphill and leap
Into new elements awaking

As I did from her sleep
    The night before my birth.

Now as I wake from a dream of death
And hear the lark invent the sun
At last I feel the thing I know
Must happen — grief begins to flow:
    Sunrise becomes earth-turn,
The thing it is; and the white deer is grazing
On Wilverley and I feel her joy
As she watched with eyes like seasons passing
    And heard the lark employ
        In song her quiet breath.

*Patrick Dickinson*


## 22. A MOTHER'S LAMENT
***FOR THE DEATH OF HER SON***

Fate gave the word, the arrow sped,
  And pierc'd my darling's heart;
And with him all the joys are fled
  Life can to me impart.

By cruel hands the sapling drops,
  In dust dishonour'd laid;
So fell the pride of all my hopes,
  My age's future shade.

The mother-linnet in the brake
  Bewails her ravish'd young;

So I, for my lost darling's sake,
 Lament the live-day long.

Death, oft I've feared thy fatal blow,
 Now, fond, I bare my breast;
O, do thou kindly lay me low
 With him I love, at rest!

Robert Burns

## 23. ON A DEAD CHILD

Perfect little body, without fault or stain on thee,
 With promise of strength and manhood full and fair!
  Though cold and stark and bare,
The bloom and the charm of life doth awhile
remain on thee.

Thy mother's treasure wert thou ; — alas! no longer
 To visit her heart with wondrous joy; to be
  Thy father's pride ; — ah, he
Must gather his faith together, and his strength
make stronger.

To me, as I move thee now in the last duty,
 Dost thou with a turn or gesture anon respond;
  Startling my fancy fond
With a chance attitude of the head, a freak of beauty.

Thy hand clasps, as 'twas wont, my finger,
and holds it:

But the grasp is the clasp of Death, heart-breaking
                                      and stiff;
          Yet feels to my hand as if
'Twas still thy will, thy pleasure and trust  that
                                      enfolds it.


So I lay thee there, thy sunken eyelids closing, —
   Go lie thou there in thy coffin, thy last little bed! —
      Propping thy wise, sad head,
Thy firm, pale hands across thy chest disposing.


So quiet ! doth the change content thee ? —
         Death, whither hath he taken thee?
   To a world, do I think, that rights the disaster of this?
      The vision of which I miss,
Who weep for the body, and wish but to warm
                              thee and awaken thee?


Ah! little at best can all our hopes avail us
   To lift this sorrow, or cheer us, when in the dark,
      Unwilling, alone we embark,
And the things we have seen and have known
              and have heard of, fail us.

*Robert Bridges*


## 24. THE WIFE A-LOST

   Since I noo mwore do zee your feäce,
      Up steäirs or down below,
   I'll zit me in the lwonesome pleäce,

Where flat-bough'd beech do grow;
Below the beeches' bough, my love,
  Where you did never come,
An' I don't look to meet ye now,
  As I do look at hwome.


Since you noo mwore be at my zide,
  In walks in zummer het,
I'll goo alwone where mist do ride,
  Drough trees a-drippen wet;
Below the raïn-wet bough, my love,
  Where you did never come,
An' I don't grieve to miss ye now,
  As I do grieve at hwome.


Since now bezide my dinner-bwoard
  Your vaïce do never sound,
I'll eat the bit I can avvword,
  A-yield upon the ground;
Below the darksome bough, my love,
  Where you did never dine,
An' I don't grieve to miss ye now,
  As I at hwome do pine.
Since I do miss your vaïce an' feäce
  In praÿer at eventide,
I'll praÿ wi' woone sad vaïcevor greäce
  To goo where you do bide;
Above the tree an' bough, my love,
  Where you be gone avore,

An' be a-waïten vor me now,
  To come vor evermwore.

William Barnes

## 25. THE WIDOW

Grief now hath pacified her face;
Even hope might share so still a place.
Yet, if — in silence of her heart —
A memoried voice or footstep start,
Or a chance word of ecstasy
Cry through dim-cloistered memory,
Into her eyes her soul will steal
To gaze on the irrevocable —
As if death had not power to keep
One, who had loved her long, so long asleep.


Now all things lovely she looks on
Wear the mute aspect of oblivion;
And all things silent seem to be
Richer than any melody.
Her narrow hands, like birds that make
A nest for some old instinct's sake,
Have hollowed a refuge for her face —
A narrow and a darkened place —
Where, far from the world's light, she may
See clearer what is passed away:
And only little children know

Through what dark half-closed gates
her smile may go.

Walter de la Mare

## 26. FOR MARK (1959)

All I held for you is wet with tears,
Dark has closed on dark,
I beat against it,
Blind in a garden without birds.

Once I sought a bright light
To guide you beyond
The Magi of my poor gifts,
But found less, much less, than fables.

You, my always son,
Will travel to my last morning,
Our hands clasped through corridors of time;
And we shall see a dawn together,
And the swallows will return.

Trevor Kneale

## 27. MIGNON II

None but whom loss has rent
Knows what I suffer.
In lonely banishment,

Dead to all pleasure,
I search the sky, intent
On one direction.
Oh! but far off he went
Who loves and knows me.
I reel; hot pangs torment
My heart and entrails.
None but whom loss has rent
Knows what I suffer.

*J. W. Goethe*
translated by Michael Hamburger


## 28.  FOR A CHILD BORN DEAD

What ceremony can we fit
You into now? If you had come
Out of a warm and noisy room
To this, there'd be an opposite
For us to know you by. We could
Imagine you in lively mood.

And then look at the other side,
The mood drawn out of you, the breath
Defeated by the power of death.
But we have never seen you stride
Ambitiously the world we know.
You could not come and yet you go.

But there is nothing now to mar
Your clear refusal of our world.

Not in our memories can we mould
You or distort your character.
Then all our consolation is
That grief can be as pure as this.

*Elizabeth Jennings*

## 29. REQUIESCAT

Strew on her roses, roses
  And never a spray of yew.
In quiet she reposes:
  Ah! would that I did too.

Her mirth the world required:
  She bath'd it in smiles of glee.
But her heart was tired, tired,
  And now they let her be.

Her life was turning, turning,
  In mazes of heat and sound.
But for peace her soul was yearning,
  And now peace laps her round.

Her cabin'd, ample Spirit,
  It flutter'd and fail'd for breath.
To-night it doth inherit
  The vast Hall of Death.

*Matthew Arnold*

# 30. REQUIESCAT

Tread lightly, she is near
Under the snow,
Speak gently, she can hear
The daisies grow.

All her bright golden hair
Tarnished with rust,
She that was young and fair
Fallen to dust.

Lily-like, white as snow,
She hardly knew
She was a woman, so
Sweetly she grew.

Coffin-board, heavy stone,
Lie on her breast,
I vex my heart alone,
She is at rest.

Peace, peace, she cannot hear
Lyre or sonnet,
All my life's buried here,
Heap earth upon it.

*Oscar Wilde*

## 31. DAY BY DAY,*
## 1940-1946

*A series of fragments written at various
times after the death of the poet's nine-
year-old son in 1939.

1.

"Noone, mother, has ever suffered so...,"
And the face already dead
But still the living eyes
Turned from the pillow towards the window,
And sparrows filled the room
Coming for the crumbs the father scattered
To distract his child...

2.

Now only in dreams will I be able
To kiss those trusting hands...
And I talk, I work,
I've scarcely changed, I smoke, I am afraid...
How is it I stand up to so much night?

3.

The years will bring me
God knows what other horrors,
But if I felt you by me
You would console me...

4.
Never, you will never know how it fills me
with light,

The shade that comes and stands beside me, shyly,
When I no longer hope...

5.

Where is it now, where is the innocent voice
That running and resounding from room to room
Raised a tired man from his troubles?…
The earth has spoilt it, it is protected by
A past of fairy tales...

6.

Every other voice is a fading echo
Now that one voice calls me
From the immortal heights…

7.

In the sky I seek your happy face,
And may these eyes of mine see nothing else
When God wills it that they too shall close…

8.

And I love you, love you, and it is an endless
                                         wrenching!…

9.

Ferocious earth, monstrous sea
Divide me from the place where the grave is
Where that tormented body
Now wastes away…
It doesn't matter… Ever more distinctly

I hear that voice of soul

That I failed to succour here below…
More joyful and more friendly
As the minutes pass,
It isolates me in its simple secret…


### 10.

I have gone back to the hills, to the  beloved pines,
And the homely accent of the wind's rhythm
That I will hear no more with you
Breaks me with every gust…


### 11.

The swallow passes and summer with her
And I too, I tell myself, will pass…
But of the love that rends me may some sign
Remain, apart from this brief misting-over,
If from this hell I reach some kind of peace…


### 12.

Under the axe the disenchanted branch
Falls with scarcely a complaint, less
Even than the leaf at the breeze's touch…
And it was fury that cut down the tender
Form, and the eager
Compassion of a voice consumes me…


### 13.

Summer brings me no more furies,
Nor spring its forebodings;
You can go your way, autumn
With your idiot splendours:

For a desire stripped bare, winter
Extends the gentlest season!…

14.

Already the drought of autumn
Has sunk into my bones,
But, drawn out by the shadows,
There survives an endless
Demented splendour:
The secret torment of the twilight buried
In an abyss…

15.

Will I always recall without remorse
A bewitching agony of the senses?
Blind man, listen: "A spirit has departed
Still unharmed by the common lash of life… "

Will I be less cast down to hear no more
The living cries of his innocence
Than to feel almost dead in me
The dreadful shudder of guilt?

16.

In the dazzle blaring from the windows
Shade frames a reflection on the tablecloth,
In the faint lustre of a jar the swollen
Hydrangeas  from the flower-bed, a drunken swift,
The skyscraper in a blaze of clouds,
A child rocking on a bough, return to mind...
Inexhaustible thunder of the waves
Forces upon me then, invades the room

And, on the uneasy stillness of a blue
Horizon, all the walls dissolve…

17.

Mild weather, and perhaps you pass close by
Saying: "May this sun and so much space
Calm you. In the pure wind you can hear
Time walking, and my voice.
Little by little I have closed and gathered
The mute impulse of your hope in me.
For you I am the dawn and the unbroken day."

*Giuseppe Ungaretti*
translated by Patrick Creagh

## 32. THE PRECEPT OF SILENCE

I know you: solitary griefs,
Desolate passions, aching hours!
I know you: tremulous beliefs,
Agonised hopes, and ashen flowers!


The winds are sometimes sad to me;
The starry spaces, full of fear:
Mine is the sorrow on the sea,
And mine the sigh of places drear.

Some players upon plaintive strings
Publish their wistfulness abroad:
I have not spoken of these things,
Save to one man, and unto God.

Lionel Johnson

## 33. A REQUIEM

It is the ritual not the fact
That brings a held emotion to
Its breaking-point. This man I knew
Only a little, by his death
Shows me a love I thought I lacked
And all the stirrings underneath.

It is the calm, the solemn thing,
Not the distracted mourners cry
Or the cold place where dead things lie,
That teaches me I cannot claim
To stand aside. These tears which sting—
Are they from sorrow or from shame?

Elizabeth Jennings

# 34. ELEGIAC VERSES

(In memory of my brother, John Wordsworth, Commander of the E. I.
Company's ship, the *Earl of Abergavenny*, in which he perished by
calamitous shipwreck, February 6, 1805.

Composed near the Mountain track, that leads to Grasmere through
Grisdale Hawes, where it descends towards Patterdale.)

I
The Sheep-boy whistled loud, and lo!
That instant, startled by the shock,
The Buzzard mounted from the rock
Deliberate and slow:

Lord of the air, he took his flight;
Oh! could he on that woeful night
Have lent his wing, my Brother dear,
For one poor moment's space to Thee,
And all who struggled with the Sea,
When safety was so near.

II
Thus in the weakness of my heart
I spoke (but let that pang be still)
When rising from the rock at will,
I saw the Bird depart.
And let me calmly bless the Power
That meets me in this unknown Flower,
Affecting type of him I mourn!
With calmness suffer and believe,

And grieve, and know that I must grieve,
Not cheerless, though forlorn.

III

Here did we stop; and here looked round
While each into himself descends,
For that last thought of parting Friends
That is not to be found.
Hidden was Grasmere Vale from sight,
Our home and his, his heart's delight,
His quiet heart's selected home.
But time before him melts away,
And he hath feeling of a day
Of blessedness to come.

IV

Full soon in sorrow did I weep,
Taught that the mutual hope was dust,
In sorrow, but for higher trust,
How miserably deep!
All vanished in a single word,
A breath, a sound, and scarcely heard.
Sea — Ship — drowned — Shipwreck —
                                       so it  came,
The meek, the brave, the good, was gone;
He who had been our living John
Was nothing but a name.

William Wordsworth

# 35.  AN OLD LAMENT RENEWED

The soil is savoury with their bones' lost  marrow;
  Down among dark roots their polished knuckles lie,
And no one could tell one peeled head from another;
  Earth packs each crater that once gleamed with eye.

Colonel and batman, emperor and assassin,
  Democratized by silence and corruption,
Defy identification with identical grin:
  The joke is long, will brook no interruption.

At night the imagination walks like a ghoul
  Among the stone lozenges and counterpanes of turf
Tumescent under cypresses; the long, rueful call
  Of the owl soars high and then wheels back to earth.

And brooding over the enormous dormitory
  The mind grows shrill at those nothings
                                        in lead rooms
Who were beautiful once or dull and ordinary,
  But loved, all loved, all called to sheltering arms.

Many I grieve with a grave, deep love
  Who are deep in the grave, whose faces I never saw:
Poets who died of alcohol, bullets, or birthdays
  Doss in the damp house, forbidden now to snore.

And in a French orchard lies whatever is left
  Of my friend, Gordon Rennie, whose courage
                                    would toughen

The muscle of resolution; he laughed
    At death's serious face, but once too often.

On summer evenings when the religious sun  stains
    The gloom in the bar and the glasses  surrender
                                    demurely
I think of Donovan whose surrender was
                                    unconditional,
    That great thirst swallowed entirely.

And often some small thing will summon the memory
    Of my small son, Benjamin. A smile  is  his
                                    sweet ghost.
But behind, in the dark, the white twig  of  his  bones
    Form a pattern of guilt and waste.

I am in mourning for the dull, the heroic and the mad;
    In the haunted nursery the child lies dead.
I mourn the hangman and his bulging complement;
    I mourn the cadaver in the egg.

The one-eyed rider aims, shoots death into the womb;
    Blood on the sheet of snow, the maiden dead.
The dagger has a double blade and meaning,
    So has the double bed.

Imagination swaggers in the sensual sun
    But night will find it at the usual mossy  gate;
The whisper from the mouldering darkness comes:
    "I am the one you love and fear and hate."

I know my grieving is made thick by terror;
  The bones of those I loved aren't fleshed by sorrow.
I mourn the deaths I've died and go on dying;
 I fear the long implacable tomorrow.

Vernon Scannell

## 36. HOLY SONNET   IV

Oh my blacke Soule! now thou art summoned
By sicknesse, deaths herald, and champion;
Thou art like a pilgrim, which abroad hath  done
Treason, and durst not turne to whence hee is fled,
Or like a thiefe, which till deaths doome be read,
Wisheth himselfe delivered from prison
But damn'd and hal'd to execution,
Wisheth that still he might be imprisoned.
Yet grace, if thou repent, thou canst not lacke
But who shall give thee that grace to beginne?
Oh make thy selfe with holy mourning blacke,
And red with blushing, as thou art with sinne;
Or wash thee in Christs blood, which hath  this might
That being red, it dyes red soules to white.

John Donne

# 37.  JOYS  THAT STING

*Oh doe not die*, says Donne, *for  I shall hate*
*All women so*. How false the sentence rings.
Women? But in a life made desolate
It is the joys once shared that have the stings.

To take the old walks alone, or not at all,
To order one pint where I ordered two,
To think of, and then not to make, the small
Time-honoured joke (senseless to all but you);

To laugh (oh, one'll laugh), to talk upon
Themes that we talked upon when you were there,
To make some poor pretence of going on,
Be kind to one's old friends, and seem to care,

While no one (O God) through the years will  say
The simplest, common word in just your way.

*C. S. Lewis*


# 38.  ECLIPSE

Loneliness will never leave you alone;
The stars are nobody's friend, but the stars  are my own.

I am nor feet nor head, but an anchored mind
That pulls at its chain in the blinded beaded  night.

A thousand miles tall, I walk on the world;
My head swims out, pulled up by the glittering stars.

I am nor guts nor heart, stretched taut
Between the soul and the heel that strikes at the mud.

They do not need me where my feet have gone;
Their tide swings in and all our friendship's  done.

I leave some words before life comes again,
That are strange music to another tongue.

Words for the happy souls to laugh about,
Who never wept so deep nor felt so hard.

Words of long death that's known before it's  come;
Loneliness will never leave you alone.

*Linette Martin*


## 39. GRIEF

O who will give me tears? Come all ye  springs,
Dwell in my head and eyes: come clouds, and rain:
My grief hath need of all the watry things,
That nature hath produc'd. Let evr'y vein
Suck up a river to supply mine eyes,
My weary weeping eyes, too drie for me,
Unlesse they get new conduits, new supplies

To bear them out, and with my state agree.
What are two shallow foords, two little spouts
Of a lesse world? the greater is but small,
A narrow cupboard for my grief's and doubts,
Which want provision in the midst of all.

Verses, ye are too fine a thing, too wise
For my rough sorrows: cease, be dumbe and mute,
Give up your feet and running to mine eyes,
And keep your measures for some lovers lute,
Whose grief allows him musick and a ryme:
For mine excludes both measure, tune,  and time.
Alas, my God!

*George Herbert*


## 40.  SECOND OPINION

We went to Leeds for a second opinion.
After her name was called,
I waited among the apparently well
And those with bandaged eyes and dark spectacles.

A heavy mother shuffled with bad feet
And a stick, a pad over one eye,
Leaving her children warned in their seats.
The minutes went by like a winter.

They called me in. What moment worse
Than that young doctor trying to explain?

"It's large and growing." "What is?" "Malignancy."
"Why there? She's an artist!"


He shrugged and said, "Nobody knows."
He warned me it might spread. "Spread?"
My body ached to suffer like her twin
And touch the cure with lips and healing sesames.


No image, no straw to support me —nothing
To hear or see. No leaves rustling in sunlight.
Only the mind sliding against events
And the antiseptic whiff of destiny.


Professional anxiety —
His hand on my shoulder
Showing me to the door, a scent of soap,
Medical fingers, and his wedding ring.

Douglas Dunn


## 41. EQUINOX

A paper cartwheels, flaps,
Drowns slowly in a pool;
Leaves descend,
Spinning orange,
Sailing red:
Graceful even in inevitable fall.

This park is a Camelot
of chilled railings
And conspiring mists;
A handclap would disturb
The huddled birds,
Strip barer still
The frieze of skeleton trees:
But gestures will not halt the equinox.


There remains declining grass,
   Soil's perceptible cooling,
Layered skies and
Easy squadrons of wild geese
Describing marvellous natural lines:
You hear only your own anguish in  their cries.

*Trevor Kneale*


## 42.  BEREFT

In the black winter morning
No light will be struck near my eyes
While the clock in the stairway is warning
For five, when he used to rise.
   Leave the door unbarred,
   The clock unwound,
   Make my lone bed hard—
   Would 'twere underground!

When the summer dawns clearly,
And the appletree-tops seem alight,
Who will undraw the curtain and cheerly
Call out that the morning is bright?

When I tarry at market
No form will cross Durnover Lea
In the gathering darkness, to hark at
Grey's Bridge for the pit-pat o' me.

When the supper crock's steaming,
And the time is the time of his tread,
I shall sit by the fire and wait dreaming
In a silence as of the dead.
    Leave the door unbarred,
    The clock unwound,
    Make my lone bed hard—
    Would 'twere underground!

*Thomas Hardy*


## 43.  A NATURAL SORROW

Silent as a falling leaf
To my heart there came a grief:
With a cold and pure despair,
Angerless, it settled there:
And must linger, and must stay,
Till it waste from mere decay,

Or till spring's uprushing tide
Thrust the skeleton aside.
I will not grudge to feel it so,
This dead leaf, this natural woe,
Neither will rage nor yet repine,
But let it lie there as a sign:
Simple as a pyramid
Where the royal dead are hid;
Naked as that ancient stone
Where *alas* is graved alone;
Humble as the tattered nest
Which once felt the thrush's breast,
And harmless as the bustling wren
That trips about it now and then.

*Ruth Pitter*


## 44. THE ABSENT

They are not here. And we, we are the Others
Who walk by ourselves unquestioned in the sun
Which shines for us and only for us.
For They are not here.
And are made known to us in this  great absence
That lies upon us and is between us
Since They are not here.
Now, in this kingdom of summer idleness
Where slowly we the sun-tranced multitudes
                                        dream and wander
In deep oblivion of brightness

And breathe ourselves out, out into the air -
It is absence that receives us;
We do not touch, our souls go out in the absence
That lies between us and is about us.
For we are the Others,
And so we sorrow for These that are not with us,
Not knowing we sorrow or that this is  our sorrow,
Since it is long past thought or memory or
                              device of mourning,
Sorrow for loss of that which we never possessed,
The unknown, the nameless,
The ever-present that in their absence are  with us
(With us the inheritors, the usurpers claiming
The sun and the kingdom of the sun) that sorrow
And loneliness might bring a blessing upon us.

*Edwin Muir*


## 45. ALONE

The abode of the nightingale is bare,
Flowered frost congeals in the gelid air,
The fox howls from his frozen lair:
        Alas, my loved one is gone,
        I am alone;
        It is winter.

Once the pink cast a winy smell,
The wild bee hung in the hyacinth bell,
Light in effulgence of beauty fell:

Alas, my loved one is gone,
I am alone;
It is winter.

My candle a silent fire doth shed,
Starry Orion hunts o'erhead;
Come moth, come shadow, the world is dead:
    Alas, my loved one is gone,
    I am alone;
    It is winter.

Walter de la Mare

## 46. THE WOUND

I climbed to the crest,
    And, fog-festooned,
The sun lay west
    Like a crimson wound:

Like that wound of mine
    Of which none knew,
For I'd given no sign
    That it pierced me through.

Thomas Hardy

## 47. MELANCHOLIA

The sickness of desire, that in dark days
Looks on the imagination of despair,

Forgetteth man, and stinteth God his praise;
Nor but in sleep findeth a cure for care.
  Incertainty that once gave scope to dream
Of laughing enterprise and glory untold,
Is now a blackness that no stars redeem,
A wall of terror in a night of cold.

  Fool! thou that hast impossibly desired
And now impatiently despairest, see
How nought is changed : Joy's wisdomis  attired
Splendid for others' eyes if not for thee

  Not love or beauty or youth from earth  is fled:
If they delite thee not, 'tis thou art dead.

*Robert Bridges*


## 48.  DREAMS

Dreams while we sleep
By reality excite
Only to disappoint
In the broadening light.
Those of the daytime
By brilliance may
Attract for a while,
As moth-like we stay
But when the flame dies,

In the afterglow
We grieve for life
We cannot know.

*Randle Manwaring*


## 49.  LARKSONG

A laverock in its house of air is singing
May morning, May morning, and its trills  drift
High on the flatland's abstract hill
In the down-below of England.
I am the aerial photograph it takes of me
On a sonar landscape
And it notates my sorrow
In Holderness, where summer frost
Melts from the green like her departing ghost.

*Douglas Dunn*


## 50.  AFTER THE FUNERAL

It is no time for tears now.
The time for tears is over.
It is the time, now.
To bar the gates.

See how the mind now
Prowls its beleaguered city,
Testing its defences, trying

Its strength, counting
Its treasure
(For there will be no more
Now the harvest is gathered)
It looks not to the plain
Where the ranked battalions of grief
Wait for the coining of night
But it knows
That the siege will be a long one
And the winter

Cold.

Evangeline Paterson

## 51.  WHO NE'ER HIS BREAD...

Who ne'er his bread with tears hath ate,
  Who never through the sad night hours
Weeping upon his bed hath sate,
  He knows not you, you heavenly powers.

Forth into life you bid us go,
  And into guilt you let us fall,
Then leave us to endure the woe
  It brings unfailingly to all.

J. W. Goethe<br>translated by A. H. Clough

# PART TWO

# STRICKEN HEART, REMEMBER

## 52.  FOR MAN ...

For man goes to his everlasting home,
 and the mourners go about the streets.

*Ecclesiastes 12.5*


## 53.  INTO MY HEART...

Into my heart an air that kills
 From yon far country blows:
What are those blue remembered hills,
 What spires, what farms are those?

That is the land of lost content,
 I see it shining plain,
The happy highways where I went
 And cannot come again.

*A. E. Housman*


## 54.  DESESPOIR

The seasons send their ruin as they go,
For in the spring the narciss shows its  head
Nor withers till the rose has flamed to red,
And in the autumn purple violets blow,

And the slim crocus stirs the winter snow
Wherefore yon leafless trees will bloom again
And this grey land grow green with summer rain
And send up cowslips for some boy to mow.

But what of life whose bitter hungry sea
Flows at our heels, and gloom of sunless  night
Covers the days which never more return?
Ambition, love and all the thoughts that  burn
We lose too soon, and only find delight
In withered husks of some dead memory.

Oscar Wilde

## 55.  REMEMBER HIM…

Remember him before the silver
cord is snapped and the golden
bowl is broken, before the pitcher
is shattered at the spring and the
wheel broken at the well, before
the dust returns to the earth as
it began and the spirit returns
to God who gave it.

Ecclesiastes 12.6-7

## 56. THE CALL

Come my heart! come my head
In sighes, and teares!

'Tis now, since you have laine thus dead
        Some twenty years;
        Awake, Awake,
        Some pitty take
        Upon your selves -
Who never wake to grone, nor weepe,
Shall be sentenc'd for their sleepe.


    Do but see your sad estate,
        How many sands
Have left us, while we careles sate
        With folded hands;
        What stock of nights,
        Of dayes, and yeares
        In silent flights
        Stole by our eares,
   How ill have we our selves bestow'd
   Whose sins are all set in a Cloud?


    Yet, come, and let's peruse them all
        And as we passe,
What sins on every minute fall
        Score on the glasse;
        Then weigh, and rate
        Their heavy State
                Untill
   The glasse with teares you fill;
   That done, we shalbe safe, and good,
   Those beasts were cleane, that chew'd the Cud.

Henry Vaughan

# 57. BITTER-SWEET

Ah, my deare angrie Lord,
Since thou dost love, yet strike;
Cast down, yet help afford;
Sure I will do the like.

I will complain, yet praise;
I will bewail, approve:
And all my sowre-sweet dayes
I will lament, and love.

*George Herbert*


# 58. THE UNQUIET GRAVE

The wind doth blow today, my love,
  And a few small drops of rain
I never had but one true-love,
  In cold grave she was lain.

I'll do as much for true-love
  As any young man may,
I'll sit and mourn all at her grave
  For a twelvemonth and a day.

The twelvemonth and a day being up,
  The dead began to speak:
Oh who sits weeping on my grave,
  And will not let me sleep?

'Tis I, my love, sits on your grave,
    And will not let you sleep,
For I crave one kiss of your clay-cold lips,
    And that is all I seek.

You crave one kiss of my clay-cold lips,
    But my breath smells earthy strong.
If you have one kiss of my clay-cold lips,
    Your time will not be long.

'Tis down in yonder garden green,
    Love, where we used to walk,
The finest flower that ere was seen
    Is withered to a stalk.

The stalk is withered dry, my love,
    So will our hearts decay.
So make yourself content, my love,
    Till God calls you away.

*Anon*


## 59.  HERE SLEEPS

Here sleeps, past earth's awakening,
A woman, true and pretty,
Who was herself in everything -
Tender, and grave, and witty.
Her smallest turn of foot, hand, head,
Was way of wind with water;

So with her thoughts and all she said -
It seemed her heart had taught her.
O thou most dear and loving soul
Think not I shall forget thee;
Nor take amiss what here is writ
For those who never met thee!

Walter de la Mare

## 60.  PARTED

Farewell to one now silenced quite,
  Sent out of hearing, out of sight,-
    My friend of friends, whom I shall miss.
    He is not banished, though, for this,-
Nor he, nor sadness, nor delight.

Though I shall talk with him no more,
A low voice sounds upon the shore.
    He must not watch my resting-place,
    But who shall drive a mournful face
From the sad winds about my door?

I shall not hear his voice complain,
But who shall stop the patient rain
    His tears must not disturb my heart,
    But who shall change the years, and part
The world from every thought of pain?

Although my life is left so dim,
The morning crowns the mountain-rim;

Joy is not gone from summer skies,

Nor innocence from children's eyes,
And all these things are part of him.

He is not banished, for the showers
Yet wake this green warm earth of ours,
How can the summer but be sweet?
I shall not have him at my feet,
And yet my feet are on the flowers.

*Alice Meynell*


## 61.  ABSENCE

I visited the place where we last met.
Nothing was changed, the gardens were well-tended,
The fountains sprayed their usual steady jet;
There was no sign that anything had ended
And nothing to instruct me to forget.

The thoughtless birds that shook out of the trees,
Singing an ecstasy I could not share,
Played cunning in my thoughts. Surely in these
Pleasures there could not be a pain to bear
Or any discord shake the level breeze.

It was because the place was just the same
That made your absence seem a savage force,

For under all the gentleness there came
An earthquake tremor: fountain, birds and grass
Were shaken by my thinking of your name.

Elizabeth Jennings


## 62.  PERHAPS...
### *To R. A. L.*

Perhaps some day the sun will shine again,
And I shall see that still the skies are blue,
And feel once more I do not live in vain,
Although bereft of You.

Perhaps the golden meadows at my feet
Will make the sunny hours of spring seem gay,
And I shall find the white May-blossoms sweet,
Though You have passed away.

Perhaps the summer woods will shimmer bright,
And crimson roses once again be fair,
And autumn harvest fields a rich delight,
Although You are not there.

But though kind Time may many joys renew,
There is one greatest joy I shall not know
Again, because my heart for loss of You
Was broken, long ago.

Vera Brittain

# 63. PAYING CALLS

I went by footpath and by stile
   Beyond where bustle ends,
Strayed here a mile and there a mile
   And called upon some friends.

On certain ones I had not seen
   For years past did I call,
And then on others who had been
   The oldest friends of all.

It was the time of midsummer
   When they had used to roam;
But now, though tempting was the air,
   I found them all at home.

I spoke to one and other of them
   By mound and stone and tree
Of things we had done ere days were  dim,
   But they spoke not to me.

*Thomas Hardy*

# 64. THE VAICES THAT BE GONE

When evenen sheädes o' trees do hide
A body by the hedge's zide,
An' twitt'ren birds, wi' plaÿsome flight,
Do vlee to roost at comen night,
Then I do saunter out o' zight
   In orcha'd,  where the pleäce woonce rung

Wi' laughs a-laugh'd an' zongs a-zung
        By vaïces that be gone.

There's still the tree that
                bore our swing,
An' others where the birds did zing;
But long-leav'd docks do overgrow
The groun' we trampled beäre below,
Wi' merry skippens to an' fro
    Bezide the banks, where Jim did zit
    A-playen o' the clarinit
        To vaïces that be gone.

How mother, when we us'd to stun
Her head wi' all our naisy fun,
Did wish us all a-gone vrom whome;
An' now that zome be dead, an'zome
A-gone, an' all the pleäce is dumb',
    How she do wish, wi' useless tears,
    To have ageän about her ears
        The vaïces that be gone.

Vor all the maidens and the bwoys
But I, be marri'd off all woys,
Or dead an' gone; but I do bide
At hwome, alwone, at mother's zide,
An' often, at the evenen-tide,
    I still do saunter out, wi' tears,
    Down drough the orcha'd, where my ears
        Do miss the vaïces gone.

William Barnes

# 65.  OVER EVERY HILL

Over every hill
All is still;
In no leaf of any tree
Can you see
The motion of a breath.
Every bird has ceased its song,
Wait; and thou too, ere long,
Shall be quiet in death.

*J. W. Goethe*
Translated by  Arthur Clough


# 66.  TALKING OF DEATH

My friend was dead. A simple sentence ended
With one black stop, like this: My friend was dead.
I had no notion that I had depended
So much on fires he lit, on that good bread
He always had to offer if I came
Hungry and cold to his inviting room.
Absurdly, I believed that he was lame
Until I started limping from his tomb.
My sorrow was the swollen, prickly kind,
Not handsome mourning smartly cut and pressed:
An actual grief, I swear. Therefore to find
Myself engaged upon a shameful quest
For anyone who'd known him, but who thought
That he was still alive, was something strange,
Something disquieting; for what I sought

Was power and presence beyond my usual range.
For once, my audience listened, welcomed me,
Avid for every syllable that spoke
Of woven fear and grieving. Nervously
They eyed my black, ambassadorial cloak.
Their faces greyed; my friend's death died, and they
Saw theirs walk in alive. I felt quite well —
Being Death's man — until they went away,
And I was left with no one else to tell.

Vernon Scannell

## 67.   THE DEATH OF THE BELOVED

He only knew of death what all men may:
that those it takes it thrusts into dumb night:
When she herself, though, — no, not snatched away,
but tenderly unloosened from his sight,

had glided over to the unknown shades,
and when he felt that he had now resigned
the moonlight of her laughter to their glades,
and all her ways of being kind:

then all at once he came to understand
the dead through her, and joined them in their walk,
kin to them all; he let the others talk,

and paid no heed to them, and called that land
the fortunately-placed, the ever-sweet. —

And groped out all its pathways for her feet.

*R. M. Rilke*
Translated by J. B. Leishman

## 68.  THE DEAD

Not because they are far, but because so near
The dead seem strange to us;
Stripped of those unprized familiar forms they wore,
Defending from our power to wound
That poignant naked thing they were,
The holy souls
Speak, essence to essence, heart  to heart.
Scarcely can we dare
To know in such intimacy
Those whom courtesy, or reticence, or fear
Hid, when, covered in skins of beasts,
Evading and evaded,
We turned the faces of our souls away.
Only the youngest child is as near as they,
Or those who share the marriage-bed
When pity and tenderness dwell there.

*Kathleen Raine*

## 69.  THE WIDOWERS

Longtime unpractised in the use
And ease of making better from worse,

As happens to old men,
Though in youth they earned a name
For singing, and a certain fame;
Yet something happens, to awaken
Unease and longing once again.

It comes too late. The power is gone,
Leaving them widowed and forsaken,
Silent in grief, for lack of breath,
The figurative skeleton
Taciturnly miming death
Behind them, while they walk away
Into the dark, out of the day.

*Richard Church*


## 70.  WIDOW

Widow. The word consumes itself —
Body, a sheet of newsprint on the fire
Levitating a numb minute in the updraft
Over the scalding, red topography
That will put her heart out like an only eye.

Widow. The dead syllable, with its shadow
Of an echo, exposes the panel in the wall
Behind which the secret passage lies --stale air,
Fusty remembrances, the coiled-spring stair
That opens at the top onto nothing at …

Widow. The bitter spider sits

And sits in the centre of her loveless spokes.
Death is the dress she wears, her hat and collar.
The moth-face of her husband, moonwhite  and ill,
Circles her like a prey she'd love to kill

A second time, to have him near again —
A paper image to lay against her heart
The way she laid his letters, till they grew warm
And seemed to give her warmth, like a live skin.
But it is she who is paper now, warmed by no-one.

Widow: that great, vacant estate!
The voice of God is full of draughtiness,
Promising simply the hard stars, the space
Of immortal blankness between stars
And no bodies, singing like arrows up to heaven.

Widow, the compassionate trees bend in,
The trees of loneliness, the trees of mourning.
They stand like shadows about the green landscape —
Or even like black holes cut out of it.
A widow resembles them, a shadow-thing,

Hand folding hand, and nothing in between.
A bodiless soul could pass another soul
In this clear air and never notice it —
One soul pass through the other, frail as smoke.
And utterly ignorant of the way it took.

That is the fear she has — the fear
His soul may beat and be beating at her dull sense
Like blue Mary's angel, dovelike against a pane

Blinded to all but the grey, spiritless room
It looks in on, and must go on looking in on.

Sylvia Plath

## 71.   AN EPITAPH

Last, Stone, a little yet;
And then this dust forget.
But thou, fair Rose, bloom on.
For she who is gone
Was lovely too; nor would she grieve to be
Sharing in solitude her dreams  with thee.

Walter de la Mare

## 72.   IF YOU HAD KNOWN

If you had known
When listening with her to the far-down moan
Of the white-selvaged and empurpled sea,
And rain came on that did not hinder talk,
Or damp your flashing facile gaiety
In turning home, despite the slow wet walk
By crooked ways, and over stiles of stone;
If you had known

You would lay roses,
Fifty years thence, on her monument, that discloses
Its graying shape upon the luxuriant green;

Fifty years thence to an hour, by chance led there,
What might have moved you? — yea, had you foreseen
That on the tomb of the selfsame one, gone where
The dawn of everyday is as the close is,
        You would lay roses!

Thomas Hardy

## 73.    THE NIGHT IS FREEZING FAST

The night is freezing fast,
    To-morrow comes December;
        And winterfalls of old
Are with me from the past;
    And chiefly I remember
        How Dick would hate the cold.

Fall, winter, fall; for he,
    Prompt hand and headpiece clever,
        Has woven a winter robe,
And made of earth and sea
    His overcoat for ever,
        And wears the turning globe.

A. E. Housman

## 74.  THE POET'S DEATH

He lay. His high-propped face could only peer
in pale rejection at the silent cover,

now that the world and all this knowledge of her,
torn from the senses of her lover,
had fallen backtothe unfeeling year.

Those who had seen him living saw no trace
of his deep unity with all that passes;
for these, these valleys here, these meadow-grasses,
these streams of running water, *were* his face.

Oh yes, his face was this remotest distance,
that seeks him still and woos him in despair;
and his mere mask, timidly dying there,
tender and open, has no more consistence
than broken fruit corrupting in the air.

*R. M. Rilke*
Translated by J. B. Leishman

## 75.   THAT TIME IS DEAD...

That time is dead for ever, child,
Drowned, frozen, dead for ever!
    we look on the past
    And stare aghast
At the spectres wailing, pale and ghast,
Of hopes which thou and I beguiled
    To death on life's dark river.

The stream we gazed on then, rolled by;
Its waves are unreturning;
    But we yet stand
    In a lone land,

Like tombs to mark the memory
Of hopes and fears, which fade and flee
In the light of life's dim morning.

Percy Bysshe Shelley

### 76.  THE MOURNERS

The boy was dead, his body lay
In the smart box.
The vicar said that death and life
compose a paradox.

Maybe. I watched the father, who
Had not seen
His son for eighteen months or more,
Face raised like a tragic queen;

Tears candidly confessed his grief,
Marched from his eyelids,
Medalled his cheeks. Some time now since
He left his wife and kids.

No histrionics from the wife,
No jewellery of tears;
She would leave for home, a cold house,
Light lamps against her fears,

Build fires against the evening chill,
And yet not cry;

Feed the living children; pray
That none of these would die.

Vernon Scannell


## 77.   THE BURIAL OF AN INFANT

Blest Infant Bud, whose Blossome-life
Did only look about, and fal,
Wearyed out in a harmles strife
Of tears, and milk, the food of all;

Sweetly didst thou expire: Thy soul
Flew home unstain'd by his new kin,
For ere thou knew'st how to be foul,
Death *wean'd* thee from the world, and sin.

Softly rest all thy Virgin-Crums!
*Lapt* in the sweets of thy young breath,
Expecting till thy Saviour Comes
To *dresse* them, and *unswaddle* death.

Henry Vaughan


## 78.  OF MY DEARE SONNE,
## GERVASE BEAUMONT

Can I, who have for others oft compil'd
The Songs of Death, forget my sweetest child,
Which like a flowr crusht, with a blast  is dead,

And ere full time hangs downe his smiling head,
Expecting with cleare hope to live anew,
Among the Angels fed with heav'nly dew?
We have this signe of Joy, that many dayes,
While on the earth his struggling spirit stayes,
The name of Jesus in his mouth containes,
His only food, his sleepe, his ease from paines.
O may that sound be rooted in my mind,
Of which in him such strong effect I find.
Deare Lord, receive my Sonne, whose winning love
To me was like a friendship, farre above
The course of nature, or his tender age,
Whose lookes could all my bitter griefes assuage;

Let his pure soule ordain'd sev'n yeares to be
In that fraile body, which was part of me,
Remaine my pledge in heav'n, as sent to shew,
How to this Port at ev'ry step I goe.

*Sir John Beaumont*
*Bosworth-Field 1629*

## 79. THAT CHILDREN IN THEIR LOVELINESS...

That children in their loveliness should die
Before the dawning beauty, which we know
Cannot remain, has yet begun to go;
That when a certain period has passed by,
People of genius and of faculty,
Leaving behind them some result to show,
Having performed some function, should forego

A task which younger hands can better ply,
Appears entirely natural. But that one
Whose perfectness did not at all consist
In things towards forming which time could  have done
Anything, — whose sole office was to exist —
Should suddenly dissolve and cease to be
Calls up the hardest questions…

*Arthur Clough*


## 80.  IN MEMORIAM F. A. S.

Yet, O stricken heart, remember, O remember
  How of human days he lived the better part.
April came to bloom and never dim December
  Breathed its killing chills upon the head or heart.

Doomed to know not Winter, only Spring, a being
  Trod the flowery April blithely for a while,
Took his fill of music, joy of thought  and seeing,
  Came and stayed and went, nor ever ceased to smile.

Came and stayed and went, and now when
                                              all is finished,
  You alone have crossed the melancholy stream,
Yours the pang, but his, O his, the  undiminished
  Undecaying gladness, undeparted dream.

All that life contains of torture, toil,  and treason,
  Shame, dishonour, death, to him were but  a name.

Here, a boy, he dwelt through all the  singing season
And ere the day of sorrow departed as he came.

*R. L. Stevenson*

## 81.   IT IS NOT GROWING LIKE A TREE

It is not growing like a tree
In bulk, doth make man better be;
Or standing long an oak, three hundred year,
To fall a log at last, dry, bald, and sere:
A lily of a day
Is fairer far, in May,
Although it fall and die that night;
It was the plant and flower of light.
In small proportions we just beauty see,
And in short measures life may perfect be.

*Ben Jonson*

## 82. TO MONICA THOUGHT DYING

You, O the piteous you!
   Who all the long night through
   Anticipatedly
   Disclose yourself to me
   Already in the ways
 Beyond our human comfortable days;
      How can you deem what Death
      Impitiably saith
      To me, who listening wake

For your poor sake?
    When a grown woman dies
You know we think unceasingly
What things she said, how sweet,  how wise;
And these do make our misery.
        But you were (you to me
The dead anticipatedly!)
You — eleven years, was't not, or so? —
        Were just a child, you know;
        And so you never said
Things sweet immeditatably and wise
To interdict from closure my wet eyes:
        But foolish things, my dead, my dead!
        Little and laughable,
        Your age that fitted well.
And was it such things all unmemorable,
        Was it such things could make
Me sob all night for your implacable sake?

        Yet, as you said to me,
In pretty make-believe of revelry,
        So the night long said Death
        With his magniloquent breath;
(And that remembered laughter,
Which in our daily uses followed after,
Was all untuned to pity and to awe:)
    *"A cup of chocolate,*
        *One farthing is the rate,*
        *You drink it through a straw."*

How could I know, how know
Those laughing words when drenched with
                              sobbing so?
Another voice than yours, than yours,  he hath.
        My dear, was't worth his breath,
His mighty utterance? — yet he saith, and saith!
This dreadful Death to his own dreadfulness
        Doth dreadful wrong,
This dreadful childish babble on his tongue.
That iron tongue made to speak sentences,
And wisdom insupportably complete,
Why should it only say the long night through,
        In mimicry of you, —
        *"A cup of chocolate,*
        *One farthing is the rate,*
*You drink it through a straw, a straw,  a straw!"*

        Oh, of all sentences,
        Piercingly incomplete!
Why did you teach that fatal mouth to draw,
        Child, impermissible awe,
        From your old trivialness?
        Why have you done me this
        Most unsustainable wrong,
        And into Death's control
Betrayed the secret places of my soul? —
        Teaching him that his lips,
Uttering their native earthquake  and eclipse,
        Could never so avail
To rend from hem to hem the ultimate veil
        Of this most desolate

Spirit, and leave it stripped and desecrate, —
        Nay, never so have wrung
From eyes and speech weakness unmanned, unmeet,
As when his terrible dotage to repeat
Its little lesson learneth at your feet;
        As when he sits among
        His sepulchres, to play
With broken toys your hand has cast away,
With derelict trinkets of the darling young.
Why have you taught —that he might  so complete
        His awful panoply
        From your cast playthings — why,
This dreadful childish babble to his tongue,
        Dreadful and sweet?

*Francis Thompson*


### 83.   THAT GOOD NIGHT

He was lying in his bed
By candle light,
Held out his hand
And smiled
And touched my face.
"Good-night " I said,
"Good-night " was his reply;
And I knew that we were friends —
Just he and I —

So gently into that good night
He quietly went his way.

Norman Machin

## 84.   AUTUMN: A DIRGE

I

The warm sun is failing, the bleak wind is wailing,
The bare boughs are sighing, the pale flowers
                           are dying,
       And the year
On the earth her deathbed, in a shroud of leaves dead,
      Is lying.
    Come, months, come away,
    From November to May,
    In your saddest array;
    Follow the bier
    Of the dead cold year,
And like dim shadows watch by her sepulchre


II

The chill rain is falling, the nipt worm is crawling,
The rivers are swelling, the thunder is knelling
      For the year;
The blithe swallows are flown, and the
                 lizards each gone
      To his dwelling;
    Come, months, come away;
    Put on white, black, and gray;

Let your light sisters play —
Ye, follow the bier
Of the dead cold year,
And make her grave green with tear on tear.

Percy Bysshe Shelley

## 85.   ABSENCE AND RETURN

### I

Do not say the rooms are empty,
  Now she is away,
Flowers and pictures decorate
  This house of clay,
Picked and painted by her hands
  In another day.

### II

How old, yet new,
Like the crocus waking in the warm
Bright air of February;
How new, yet old,
Like a tune long forgotten,
Played again...

Randle Manwaring

## 86.   THE LITTLE OLD TABLE

Creak, little wood thing, creak,

When I touch you with elbow or knee;
That is the way you speak
Of one who gave you to me!

You, little table, she brought —
Brought me with her own hand,
As she looked at me with a thought
That I did not understand.

— Whoever owns it anon,
And hears it, will never know
What a history hangs upon
This creak from long ago.

Thomas Hardy

## 87.  FOR SALE

Death's slow paralysis
Over him stole,
Ashen-grey, bent
In body and soul.

His house, like his frame,
Quite empty lies;
Vanished the light
From windows and eyes.

The creeper is black
On the stucco wall

81

And the holland blinds
Allowed to fall.

To the shrivelled past
Of life's history
He hastened there
Dying to be,

Joining the glories
He was loathe to forsake
Whilst of his detached villa
Two flats will they make.

Randle Manwaring

## 88.  AWAY

There is no sorrow
Time heals never;
No loss, betrayal,
Beyond repair.
Balm for the soul, then,
Though grave shall sever
Lover from loved
And all they share;
See, the sweet sun shines,
The shower is over,
Flowers preen their beauty,
The day how fair!
Brood not too closely
On love, or duty;

Friends long forgotten
May wait you where
Life with death
Brings all to an issue;
None will long mourn for you,
Pray for you, miss you,
Your place left vacant,
You not there.

Walter de la Mare

## 89.  MARY

Her name was poet's grief before
Mary, the saddest name
In all the litanies of love
And all the books of fame.

I think of poor John Clare's beloved
And know the blessed pain
When crusts of death are broken
And tears are blossomed rain.

And why should I lament the wind
Of chance that brought her here
To be an April offering
For sins my heart held dear.

And though her passing was for me
The death of something sweet,

Her name's in every prayer, her charm
In every face I meet.
*Patric Kavanagh*

## 90. ELEGY

Her face like a rain-beaten stone on the day
she rolled off
With the dark hearse, and enough flowers for
an alderman, —
And so she was, in her way, Aunt Tilly.

Sighs, sighs, who says they have sequence?
Between the spirit and the flesh, —
what war?
She never knew;
For she asked no quarter and gave none,
Who sat with the dead when the relatives left,
Who fed and tended the infirm, the mad,  the epileptic,
And, with a harsh rasp of a laugh at herself,
Faced up to the worst.

I recall how she harried the children away all
the late summer
From the one beautiful thing in her yard,  the peachtree;
How she kept the wizened, the fallen, the misshapen
for herself,
And picked and pickled the best, to be left on
rickety doorsteps.

And yet she died in agony,
Her tongue, at the last, thick, black as an ox's.

Terror of cops, bill collectors, betrayers  of the poor, —
 I see you in some celestial supermarket,
Moving serenely among the leeks and cabbages,
Probing the squash,
Bearing down, with two steady eyes,
On the quaking butcher.

*Theodore Roethke*


## 91.  THE COCK'S NEST

The spring my father died — it was  winter, really,
February fill-grave, but March was in
Before we felt the bruise of it and knew
 How empty the rooms were — that spring
A wren flew to our yard, over Walter Willson's
Warehouse roof and the girls' school  playground
From the old allotments that are now no more
                              than a compost
For raising dockens and cats. It found a niche
Tucked behind the pipe of the bathroom outflow,
Caged in a wickerwork of creeper; then
Began to build:
Three times a minute, hour after hour,
Backward and forward to the backyard wall,
Nipping off neb-fulls of the soot-spored moss
Rooted between the bricks. In a few days
The nest was finished. They say the cock
Leases an option of sites and leaves the hen
To choose which nest she will. She didn't choose
                              our yard.

And as March gambolled out, the fat King-Alfred sun
Blared down too early from its tinny trumpet
On new-dug potato-beds, the still bare creeper,
The cock's nest with never an egg in,
And my father dead.

Norman Nicholson

## 92.  MAY AND DEATH

### I.

I wish that when you died last May,
   Charles, there had died along with you
Three parts of spring's delightful things;
   Ay, and, for me, the fourth part too.

### II.

A foolish thought, and worse, perhaps!
   There must be many a pair of friends
Who, arm in arm, deserve the warm
   Moon-births and the long evening-ends.

### III.

So, for their sake, be May still May!
   Let their new time, as mine of old,
Do all it did for me: I bid
   Sweet sights and sounds throng manifold.

### IV.

Only, one little sight, one plant,
   Woods have in May, that starts up green

Save a sole streak which, so to speak,
   Is spring's blood, spilt its leaves  between, —

V.

That, they might spare; a certain wood
   Might miss the plant; their loss were small;
But I, — whene'er the leaf grows there,
   Its drop comes from my heart, that's all.

*Robert Browning*

## 93. FOR COUNT KARL LANCKORONSKI

*"No intellect,  no ardour is  reduntant"* :
to make one through the other more abundant
is what we're for, and some are singled out
for purest victory in that contention:
no signal can escape their tried attention,
their hands are wieldy and their weapons  stout.

No sound must be too soft for their detection,
they must perceive that angle of deflection
to which the dial-pointer scarcely stirs,
and must, as might be with their eyelids, utter
reply to what the butterflies out-flutter
and learn to fathom what a flower infers.

No less than others they can be extinguished,
and yet they must (why else were they distinguished?)
feel even with catastrophe some kin,
and, while the rest are helplessly bewailing,

recapture in the strokes of each assailing
the rhythm of some stoniness within.
They must be stationed like a shepherd, keeping
his lonely watch: one might suppose him weeping,
till, coming close, one feels his piercing sight;
and, as as for him speech of stars is clear,
for them must be as intimately near
what climbs in still procession through the night.

In slumber also they continue seers:
from dream and being, from laughter and from tears
a meaning gathers... which if they can seize,
and kneel to Life and Death in adoration,
another measure for the whole creation
is given us in those right-angled knees.

*R. M. Rilke*
Translated by J. B. Leishman

## 94.  ASLEEP

Under his helmet, up against his pack,
Alter the many days of work and waking,
Sleep took him by the brow and laid him back.
And in the happy no-time of his sleeping,
Death took him by the heart. There was  a quaking
Of the aborted life within him leaping ...
Then chest and sleepy arms once more fell slack.
And soon the slow, stray blood came creeping
From the intrusive lead, like ants on track.

.     .     .     .     .     .

Whether his deeper sleep lie shaded the shaking
Of great wings, and the thoughts that hung the stars,
High-pillowed on calm pillows of God's making
Above these clouds, these rains, these sleets of lead,
And these winds' scimitars;
— Or whether yet his thin and sodden head
Confuses more and more with the low mould,
His hair being one with the grey grass
And finished fields of autumns that are old …
Who knows? Who hopes? Who troubles? Let it pass!
He sleeps. He sleeps less tremulous, less cold,
Than we who must awake, and waking, say Alas!

*Wilfred Owen*


## 95.　AUGURIES OF LIFE AND DEATH
*(In memory of Charles Read, 1897-1918)*

1.

The autumn leaves were an augury
And seemed to intend
As they yellowly drooped in the languid air
That life was a fragile mood and death
A tremendous despair.

The yellow leaves fell
Like slow tears of gold on the face of the day:
They fell to the earth with a faint sad sigh.

They sighed
As the feet of the passers-by
Crushed them into the moist black soil:
They sighed when the gentle wind
Lifted them along the way.

In the park
Old men swept the dead things in a heap to burn:
Their last fragrance
Floated about the naked trees.

I thought as the women walked in the
                              moist still day
Wearing yellow chrysanthemums in their coats
A chrysanthemum was
A pale dishevelled emblem of death.

The sun
Was a silver pervasion across  the sky:
From the sky
The dead leaves fell.

2..

Some well-meaning fool
called him an unconscious Sidney
proudly dying in the surge of battle.
Many said
he paid the supreme sacrifice....

Let us be frank for once:
Such foisted platitudes
cannot console sick hearts.

Rather this alone is clear:
He was a delightful youth
irradiating joy, peculiarly loved
by hundreds of his fellows.
The impulse of his living
left a wake of laughter
and happiness in the hearts of sad men.

Then this glad progression
is suddenly cut short
annihilated.
We hear
he was killed in action, leading his men…
In a moment that life and its radiance
went out like a blown flame.

No natural logic can explain
that harsh departure and our dark void.
The knotted bitterness grips tight
I curse the fate that sent us
a tortured species down the torrent of life
soul-exposed to insensate shores
and the dark fall of death.

Yet in the scene of life
a consolation I can find.
All things do cry
vain is rebellion.
Is not the gargoyle leer of fate
in all its impassive cruelty
known too well
for any man to rebel?

The tendrils of our intensest emotions
are torn by its inane force
and strewn in bleeding death.
But no devastation can
utterly kill:
in the burnt blackness of earth
built from invisible beginnings
womb-warmth will engender
an animate thing.


So we might make his short delightful life
an instance of those beauties that adorn
tragically the earth with flowers
heroes and valiant hearts.
This flower hold dear
till the years evolve in their callous  recession
a memorized beauty.


3.

All the world is wet with tears
and droops its languid life
in sympathy.
But death is beautiful with pride: the trees
are golden lances whose brave array
assails the sadness of the day.
They do not meet
fate with an angry tumult:
Serene they stay
austerely dying day by day:
Their golden lances imperceptibly fade

into the sleep of winter, their victory made
in the hearts of men.

Herbert Read


## 96.  FRAGMENT: "IT IS NOT DEATH"

It is not death
    Without hereafter
To one in dearth
    Of life and its laughter,

Nor the sweet murder
    Dealt slow and even
Unto the martyr
    Smiling at heaven:

It is the smile
    Faint as a [waning] myth,
Faint, and exceeding small
    On a boy's murdered mouth. -

Wilfred Owen


## 97.  PINE FOREST
(In memoriam — K.A.M.W.)

Among the towering pines
of perennial pride,
falling but not fallen,

the mossy path astride,
adding a new dimension,
one leans across the ride.

Caught at sixty degrees
it makes a special mark
with shafts of angled light
in the criss-cross dark,
dead amongst the living,
lying bark to bark.

When will it fall completely,
all support withdrawn
by neighbour pines,
their roots outworn,
on a brushwood couch
to be stripped and sawn?

We stand together now,
silent among the trees,
wondering at the limit
of life's harmonies,
as the wind, passing over,
another death decrees.

*Randle Manwaring*


## 98. WAYSIDE CRUCIFIX

A tank lies gutted in the ditch beneath...
English or German? That's no matter now;

The pinioned Man with thorns upon His brow
Looks down upon a grave that bears no wreath,
Beside the wrecked and blackened iron sheath.
The toil-bent peasant leaves his healing plough
To gaze upon the Sacrifice and bow
His head, pond'ring the gift that guns bequeath
Unto his ravaged soil: the human clay
Moulded from other dust — and hither brought
To jest and suffer for a space, to slay
And mingle with an alien earth,  blood-bought.
The slain will guard the slain till Rising Day
When he shall know the End for which he fought.

*L. E. S. Cotterell*


## 99. STRANGE MEETING

It seemed that out of battle I escaped
Down some profound dull tunnel, long since scooped
Through granites which titanic wars  had groined.
Yet also there encumbered sleepers groaned,
Too fast in thought or death to be bestirred.
Then, as I probed them, one sprang, and stared
With piteous recognition in fixed eyes,
Lifting distressful hands as if to bless.
And by his smile, I knew that sullen hall,
By his dead smile I knew we stood in Hell.
With a thousand pains that vision's face was grained;
Yet no blood reached there from the upper ground,
And no guns thumped, or down the flues made moan.
"Strange friend," I said, "here is no cause to mourn."

"None," said the other, "save the undone years,
The hopelessness. Whatever hope is yours,
Was my life also; I went hunting wild
After the wildest beauty in the world,
Which lies not calm in eyes, or braided hair,
But mocks the steady running of the hour,


And if it grieves, grieves richlier than here.
For by my glee might many men have laughed,
And of my weeping something had been left,
Which must die now. I mean the truth untold,
The pity of war, the pity war distilled.
Now men will go content with what we spoiled.
Or, discontent, boil bloody, and be spilled.
They will be swift with swiftness of the tigress
None will break ranks, though nations trek from
                                        progress.
Courage was mine, and I had mystery,
Wisdom was mine, and I had mastery;
To miss the march of this retreating world
Into vain citadels that are not walled.
Then, when much blood had clogged their
                                    chariot-wheels
I would go up and wash them from sweet wells,
Even with truths that lie too deep for taint.
I would have poured my spirit without stint
But not through wounds; not on the cess of war.
Foreheads of men have bled where nowounds were.
I am the enemy you killed, my friend.
I knew you in this dark; for so you frowned
Yesterday through me as you jabbed and killed.

I parried; but my hands were loath and cold.
Let us sleep now…"

Wilfred Owen

## 100.  TO KNOW…

To know just how He suffered —would be dear —
To know if any Human eyes were near
To whom He could entrust His wavering gaze —
Until it settled broad — on Paradise —

To know if He was patient —part content —
Was Dying as He thought — or different —
Was it a pleasant Day to die —
And did the Sunshine face His way —

What was His furthest mind — Of Home — or God —

Or what the Distant say —
At news that He ceased Human Nature
Such a Day —

And Wishes — Had He Any —
Just His Sigh — Accented —
Had been legible — to Me —
And was He Confident until
Ill fluttered out — in Everlasting Well —

And if He spoke — What name was Best —
What last

What One broke off with
At the Drowsiest —

Was He afraid — or  tranquil —
Might He know
How Conscious Consciousness — could grow —
Till Love that was — and Love too best to be —
Meet — and the Junction be Eternity

Emily Dickinson

## 101.  JOY AND GRIEF

What of my Joy?
See how she fades;
While Grief, great growing boy,
Devours, invades;
He my whole having eats,
She finds no food,
And by my chimney sits
In dying attitude.

When she is gone
With Grief I'll dwell;
When we are left alone,
He, who can tell?
May gentler grow, and be
In my cold age
A comforter to me,
The wounds he gave, assuage.

Meanwhile I nourish both,
The devourer and the dying:
I am strong, I cast away sloth
And do but little sighing;
See the sad purity
Of the white sky and the stream!
On these, and the winter tree,
I will gaze, I will dream.

Ruth Pitter

## 102.  ONE GRIEF OF THINE

One grief of thine
   if truth be confest
Was joy to me;
   for it drave to my breast
Thee, to my heart
   to find thy rest

How long it was
   I never shall know:
I watcht the earth
   so stately and slow,
And the ancient things
   that waste and grow.

But now for me
   what speed devours

Our heavenly life,
    our brilliant hours!
How fast they fly,
    the stars and flowers!

*Robert Bridges*

# PART THREE

# NO SADNESS OF FAREWELL

## 103.  *From* GITANJALI

On the day when death will knock at
thy door what wilt thou offer to him?
   Oh, I will set before my guest the
full vessel of my life — I will never
let him go with empty hands.
   All the sweet vintage of all my
autumn days and summer nights, all
the earnings and gleanings of my busy
life will I place before him at the
close of my days when death will knock
at my door.

*Rabindranath Tagore*


## 104.  *From* QUIET MOMENT

"Deliver me from my own shadows, my Lord,
   from the wrecks and confusion of my days,
For the night is dark and Thy pilgrim is  blinded;
Hold Thou my hand.
Deliver me from despair.

Touch with Thy flame the lightless lamp
of my sorrow.
Waken my tired strength from its sleep.
Do not let me linger behind counting my losses.


For the night is dark and Thy pilgrim is blinded;
Hold Thou my hand."

Rabindranath Tagore


## 105.  THE WAYFARERS

Is it the hour? We leave this resting-place
  Made fair by one another for a while.
Now, for a god-speed, one last mad embrace;
  The long road then, unlit by your faint  smile.
Ah!the long road! and you so far away!
  Oh, I'll remember! but…crawling day
Will pale a little your scarlet lips,  each mile
  Dull the dear pain of your remembed face.

…Do you think there's a far border town,  somewhere,
  The desert's edge, last of the lands  we know,
    Some gaunt eventual limit of our light,
  In which I'll find you waiting; and we'll go
Together, hand in hand again, out there,
  Into the waste we know not, into the night?

Rupert  Brooke

# 106. I HAVE GOT MY LEAVE

I have got my leave. Bid me farewell,
my brothers! I bow to you all and take
my departure.
   Here I give back the keys of my  door —
and I give up all claims to my house. I only
ask for last kind words from you.
   We were neighbours for long, but  I received
more than I could give.
Now the day has dawned and the lamp that
lit my dark corner is out. A summons has come
and I am ready for my journey.

*Rabindranath Tagore*

# 107.  FARE WELL

When I lie where shades of darkness
Shall no more assail mine eyes,
Nor the rain make lamentation
     When the wind sighs;
How will fare the world whose wonder
Was the very proof of me?
Memory fades, must the remembered
     Perishing be?

Oh, when this my dust surrenders
Hand, foot, lip, to dust again,

May these loved and loving faces
        Please other men!
May the rusting harvest hedgerow
Still the Traveller's Joy entwine;

And as happy children gather
        Posies once mine.

Look thy last on all things lovely,
Every hour. Let no night
Seal thy sense in deathly slumber
        Till to delight
Thou have paid thy utmost blessing;
Since that all things thou wouldst praise
Beauty took from those who loved them
        In other days.

*Walter de la Mare*


## 108.  SONNET

Remember me when I am gone away,
   Gone far away into the silent land;
   When you can no more hold me by the  hand,
Nor I half turn to go yet turning stay.
   Remember me when no more day by day
   You tell me of our future that you planned:
   Only remember me; you understand
It will be late to counsel then or pray.
   Yet if you should forget me for a while
   And afterwards remember, do not grieve:

For if the darkness and corruption leave
A vestige of the thoughts that once I had,
Better by far you should forget   and smile
Than that you should remembe and be sad.


*Christina Rossetti*

## 109.  THE BRIDGE

Where is the truth that will inform my sorrow?
I am sure myself that sorrow is not the truth.
These lovely shapes of sorrow are empty vessels
Waiting for wine: they wait to be informed.
Men make the vessels on either side of the river;
On this the hither side the artists make them,
And there over the water the workmen make them:
These frail, with a peacock glaze, and the others heavy,
Simple as doom, made to endure the furnace.
War shatters the peacock-jars: let us go over.

Indeed we have no choice but to go over.

There is always a way for those who must go over:
Always a bridge from the known to the unknown.
When from the known the mind revolts and despairs
There lies the way, and there we must go over.

O truth, is it death there over the river,
Or is it life, new life in a land of summer?
The mind is an empty vessel, a shape of  sorrow,
Fill it with life or death, for it is hollow,

Dark wine or bright, fill it, let us go over.
Let me go find my truth, over the river.

*Ruth Pitter*

## 110. FALLING LEAVES

Whirled dust, world dust,
Tossed and torn from trees,
No more they labour for life, no more
Shelter of green glade, shade
Of apples under leaf, lifted in air
They soar, no longer leaves.

What, wind that bears me,
Am I about to be? Will water
Draw me down among its multitude?
Earth shall I return, shall I return to the tree?
Or by fire go further
From myself than now I can know or dare?

*Kathleen Raine*

## 111.  A SHADOW

I said unto myself, if I were dead,
  What would befall these children? What  would be
Their fate,who now are looking up to me
  For help and furtherance? Their lives,  I said,
Would be a volume wherein I have read

But the first chapters, and no longer see
To read the rest of their dear history,
So full of beauty and so full of dread.
Be comforted; the world is very old,
And generations pass, as they have passed,
A troop of shadows moving with the sun;
Thousands of times has the old tale  been told;
The world belongs to those who come  the last,
They will find hope and strength as we have done.

*H. W. Longfellow*


## 112.  SONNET

When I have fears that I may cease to be
Before my pen has glean'd my teeming brain,
Before high-piled books, in charactery,
Hold like rich garners the full ripen'd grain;
When I behold, upon the night's starr'd face,
Huge cloudy symbols of a high romance,
And think that I may never live to trace
Their shadows, with the magic hand of chance;
And when I feel, fair creature of an hour,
That I shall never look upon thee more,
Never have relish in the faery power
Of unreflecting love — then on the shore
Of the wide world I stand alone, and think
Till love and fame to nothingness do sink.

*John Keats*

# 113.  THE OLD MAN DYING

The old woman sits with drooping mouth
waiting for the old man
to live again.
He lies in his red wing armchair,
brocade, flustered and tatty.
His sighs are regular and swell
to moans.
Don't listen to him, he's putting it on.
And she turns him
and feeds him on baby foods.
When his brain swings back
a cell at a time, at twilight
for ten minutes before his bedtime,
her cynic's face goes tender,
eyes under the hooded chalky lids
brighten.
Daddy is good today. He's better. See!
He turns his bald head on its dew-lap
like a tortoise, nosing
for sun. Later he sleeps.
She wipes the dribble from his lips
and heaving and panting, corseted, small,
she carefully beds him for the night,
All night she patchily sleeps,
her thick back aches, and
she listens for his moans, and for the change
of breath, the elusive and dreadful
departure.

*Judith Kazantzis*

## 114. THE LIFE THAT I HAVE —

The Life that I have
Is all that I have
And the life that I have
Is yours
The love that I have
Of the life that I have
Is yours, and yours, and yours.
A sleep I shall have
A rest I shall have
Yet death will be but a pause,
For the peace of my years
In the long green grass
Will be yours, and yours, and yours.

*Leo Marks*


## 115. AT SIXTY

If you walk backwards towards death
Like water flowing uphill,
Suddenly the world you'll never know
(Nor that world know that it lack you)

Will rattle by in a rush
Of prams and the beautiful young
Will saunter beside a building
Outstanding your possession,

Saunter and will not glance
At your uphill motion;
Now is the time to go
Two ways at once.

To the spring of your bones,
And on to dissolution;
Aware more of the mayfly
Than the worlds of flesh and stone,

And catch the children's eyes whose suns
Will make their shadows taller,
And turn into the sun
Till you have no shadow at all.

Patrick Dickinson

## 116.  TELL ME NOT HERE —

Tell me not here, it needs not saying,
   What tune the enchantress plays
In aftermaths of soft September
   Or under blanching mays,
For she and I were long acquainted
   And I knew all her ways.

On russet floors, by waters idle,
   The pine lets fall its cone;
The cuckoo shouts all day at nothing
   In leafy dells alone;

And traveller's joy beguiles in autumn
   Hearts that have lost their own.

On acres of the seeded grasses
   The changing burnish heaves;
Or marshalled under moons of harvest
   Stand still all night the sheaves;
Or beeches strip in storms for winter
   And stain the wind with leaves.

Possess, as I possessed a season,
   The countries I resign,
Where over elmy plains the highway
   Would mount the hills and shine,
And full of shade the pillared forest
   Would murmur and be mine.

For nature, heartless, witless nature,
   Will neither  care nor know
What stranger's feet may find the meadow
   And trespass there and go,
Nor ask amid the dews of morning
   If they are mine or no.

*A. E. Housman*


## 117. THE DEBT

I owe so large a debt to life,
I think if I should die to-day

My death would never quite repay
For music, friends and careless laughter,
The swift, light-hearted interplay
Of wit on ready wit, and after,
The silence that most blessed falls
Across the room and firelit walls
And quells our flame of jesting strife.
I owe so large a debt to life
No gift can wipe it quite away,
Nor any tears that I can borrow
From watching all the world's  wild sorrow,
As Autumn never can allay
The promise of a sunlit morrow
We had as legacy from May.

Winifred Holtby

## 118.  SONNET 71

No longer mourn for me when I am dead
Than you shall hear the surly sullen bell
Give warning to the world that I am fled
From this vile world, with vilest worms to dwell;
Nay, if you read this line, remember not
The hand that writ it; for I love you so,
That I in your sweet thoughts would be forgot,
If thinking on me then should make you woe.
O, if, I say, you look upon this verse
When I perhaps compounded am with clay,
Do not so much as my poor name rehearse,
But let your love even with my life decay;

Lest the wise world should look into your moan,
And mock you with me after I am gone.

William Shakespeare

## 119. INDIAN PRAYER *(traditional)*

When I am dead
Cry for me a little
Think of me sometimes
But not too much.
Think of me now and again
As I was in life
At some moments it's pleasant to recall
But not for long.
Leave me in peace
And I shall leave you in peace
And while you live
Let your thoughts be with the living.

Anon

## 120. *From* IN MEMORIAM

### 50.

Be near me when my light is low,
  When the blood creeps, and the nerves  prick
  And tingle; and the heart is sick,
And all the wheels of Being slow.

Be near me when the sensuous frame
  Is rack'd with pangs that conquer trust;
  And Time, a maniac scattering dust,
And Life, a Fury slinging flame.

Be near me when my faith is dry,
  And men the flies of latter spring,
  That lay their eggs, and sting and sing
And weave their petty cells and die.

Be near me when I fade away,
  To point the term of human strife,
  And on the low dark verge of life
The twilight of eternal day.


# 51.

Do we indeed desire the dead
  Should still be near us at our side?
  Is there no baseness we would hide?
No inner vileness that we dread?

Shall he for whose applause I strove,
  I had such reverence for his blame,
  See with clear eye some hidden shame
And I be lessen'd in his love?

I wrong the grave with fears untrue:
  Shall love be blamed for want of faith?
  There must be wisdom with great Death:
The dead shall look me thro' and thro'.

Be near us when we climb or fall:
    Ye watch, like God, the rolling hours
    With larger other eyes than ours,
To make allowance for us all.

Alfred, Lord Tennyson

## 121.  IN A DARK TIME

In a dark time, the eye begins to see,
I meet my shadow in the deepening shade;
I hear my echo in the echoing wood —
A lord of nature weeping to a tree.
I live between the heron and the wren,
Beasts of the hill and serpents of the den.

What's madness but nobility of soul
At odds with circumstance? The day's  on fire!
I know the purity of pure despair,
My shadow pinned against a sweating wall.
That place among the rocks — is it a cave,
Or winding path? The edge is what I have.

A steady storm of correspondences!
A night flowing with birds, a ragged moon,
And in broad day the midnight come again!
A man goes far to find out what he is —
Death of the self in a long, tearless  night,
All natural shapes blazing unnatural light.

Dark, dark my light, and darker my desire.
My soul, like some heat-maddened summer fly,
Keeps buzzing at the sill. Which I is *I*?
A fallen man, I climb out of my fear.
The mind enters itself, and God the mind,
And one is One, free in the tearing wind.

*Theodore Roethke*


## 122. SONNET 66

Tired with all these, for restful death I cry,
As, to behold desert a beggar born,
And needy nothing trimm'd in jollity,
And purest faith unhappily forsworn,
And gilded honour shamefully misplaced,
And maiden virtue rudely strumpeted,
And right perfection wrongfully disgraced,
And strength by limping sway disabled,
And art made tongue-tied by authority,
And folly, doctor-like, controlling skill,
And simple truth miscall'd simplicity,
And captive good attending captain ill:
  Tired with all these, from these would I be gone,
  Save that, to die, I leave my love alone.

*William Shakespeare*

# 123. CANZONE

Ah me! ah me! when thinking of the years,
The vanished years, alas, I do not find
Among them all one day that was my own!
Fallacious hopes, desires of the unknown,
Lamenting, loving, burning, and in tears
(For human passions all have stirred my mind),
Have held me, now I feel and know, confined
Both from the true and good still far away.
I perish day by day;

The sunshine fails, the shadows grow more  dreary,
And I am near to fall, infirm and weary.

*Henry W. Longfellow*


# 124. OH DEATH TREAD SOFTLY

Oh death
I have such
Mixed feelings
For you
Sometimes
I dread you
Sometimes
I await thee
I know not
When
Thou shalt embrace me

Oh, death
I do have a favour to ask thee
When thou comest
Oh, please dear death
Do come but
Unannounced
For there are crushed hearts
Within these walls
Hearts that love, adore and care
Hearts that bleed
Inwardly

And show not a care
But they do care
For the one
Whom you await to claim
Let them be asleep
Or take me in my slumber
For partings are so painful
Especially for those
Who reared me…
From a seeding to a flower

Oh death
Tread softly
For I fear for those
Who fear for me
Do not be very harsh
Spare me, oh please spare me
Little suffering
Spare me a little pain
And please spare me just a…

Few tears
To shed them
In the presence of God
To show HIM my gratitude
For after all isn't HE
Sparing me
From this cruel, cruel world
Where there are
Some people
Who don't even have a heart.

Gitanjali Badruddin

## 125.  IN THE MIDST OF LIFE

Death and I are only nodding acquaintances
We have not been formally introduced
But many times I have noticed
The final encounter
Here in this hospice,
I can truly say
That death has been met with dignity
Who can divine the thoughts
Of a man in close confrontation?
I can only remember
One particular passing
When a man,
With sustained smile
Pointed out what was for him
Evidently a great light
Who knows what final revelations
Are received in the last hours?

Lord, grant me a star in the East
As well as a smouldering sunset.

Sidney G. Reeman

## 126.  THE JUDGEMENT DAY

God hides from man the reckoning Day,  that He
May feare it ever for uncertaintie:
That being ignorant of that one, he may

Expect the coming of it ev'ry day.

Robert Herrick

## 127.  WHEN I AM COVERED

When I am covered with the dust of peace
And but the rain to moist my senseless clay,
Will there be one regret left in that ill ease

One sentimental fib of light and day-
A grief for hillside and the beaten trees?
Better to leave them, utterly to go away.

When every tiny pang of love is counterpiece
To shadowed woe of huge weight and the stay
For yet another torment ere release

Better to lie and be forgotten aye.
In Death his rose-leaves never is a crease.
Rest squares reckonings Love set awry.

Ivor Gurney


## 128.  THE CAGED GOLDFINCH

Within a churchyard, on a recent grave,
    I saw a little cage


That jailed a goldfinch. All was silence save
    Its hops from stage to stage.

There was inquiry in its wistful eye,
    And once it tried to sing;
Of him or her who placed it there, and why,
    No one knew anything.

Thomas Hardy


## 129.  THE FALL OF THE LEAF

The lazy mist hangs from the brow of the hill,
Concealing the course of the dark winding rill;
How languid the scenes, late so sprightly,  appear,
As Autumn to Winter resigns the pale year!

The forests are leafless, the meadows are brown,

And all the gay foppery of summer is flown:
Apart let me wander, apart let me muse,
How quick Time is flying, how keen Fate  pursues!

How long I have liv'd — but how much liv'd in vain,
How little of life's scanty span may remain,
What aspects old Time in his progress  has worn,
What ties cruel Fate in my bosom has torn.

How foolish, or worse, till our summit is gain'd!
And downward, how weaken'd, how darken'd,
                                        how pain'd!

Life is not worth having with all it can give —
For something beyond it poor man sure must live.

Robert Burns

## 130.  SONNET 146

Poor soul, the centre of my sinful earth,
…these rebel Powers that thee array,
Why dost thou pine within and suffer dearth,
Painting thy outward walls so costly gay?
Why so large cost, having so short a lease,
Dost thou upon thy fading mansion spend?
Shall worms, inheritors of this excess,
Eat up thy charge? is this thy body's end?
Then, soul, live thou upon thy servant's loss,
And let that pine to aggravate thy store;
Buy terms divine in selling hours of dross

Within be fed, without be rich no more :
    So shalt thou feed on Death, that feeds  on men,
    And Death once dead, there's no more dying then.

William Shakespeare

## 131.  MOMENTS

I think the loathed minutes one by one
That tear and then go past are little worth
Save nearer to the blindness to the sun
They bring me, and the farewell to all earth.
Save to that six-foot-length I must lie in
Sodden with mud, and not to grieve again
Because high Autumn goes beyond my pen
And snow lies inexprest in the deep lane.

Ivor Gurney

## 132.  THE THEME OF DEATH

Since love is an astonished always
Challenging the long lies of history,
Yesterday when I chose the theme of death
You shook a passionate finger at me:
"Wake from your nightmare! Would you murder love?
Wake from your nightmare!"

No, sweetheart! Death is nightmare when conceived
As God's Last Judgement, or the curse of Time —

Its intransgressible bounds of destiny;
But love is an astonished always
With death as affidavit for its birth
 And timeless progress.

What if these tombs and catafalques conspire,
Menacing us with gross ancestral fears,
To dissipate my living truth, and yours,
To induct us into ritual weeping?
Our love remains a still astonished always,
    Pure death its witness.

Robert Graves

## 133. INFIRMITY

In purest song one plays the constant fool
As changes shimmer in the inner eye.
I stare and stare into a deepening pool
And tell myself my image cannot die.
I love myself: that's my one constancy.
Oh, to be something else, yet still to be!


Sweet Christ, rejoice in my infirmity;
There's little left I care to call my own.
Today they drained the fluid from a knee
And pumped a shoulder full of cortisone;
Thus I conform to my divinity
By dying inward, like an ageing tree.

The instant ages on the living eye;
Light on its rounds, a pure extreme of light
Breaks on me as my meagre flesh breaks  down —
The soul delights in that extremity.
Blessed the meek; they shall inherit wrath;
I'm son and father of my only death.

A mind too active is no mind at all;
The deep eye sees the shimmer on the stone;
The eternal seeks, and finds, the temporal,
The change from dark to light of the  slow moon,
Dead to myself, and all I hold most dear,
I move beyond the reach of wind and fire.

Deep in the greens of summer sing the lives
I've come to love. A vireo whets its bill.
The great day balances upon the leaves;
My ears still hear the bird when all is still;
My soul is still my soul, and still the Son,
And knowing this, I am not yet undone.

Things without hands take hands:
                              there is no choice —
Eternity's not easily come by.
When opposites come suddenly in place,
I teach my eyes to hear, my ears to see
How body from spirit slowly does unwind
Until we are pure spirit at the end.

Theodore Roethke

# 134. THE FRAGILE THREAD

Life is like a
Fragile thread
One does not know
When it might snap

The only solid
Hold on it
Is the faith
That is…
If
You trust and care

Be prepared
To face death
As and when
She appears
Death is like a
Honoured guest
She comes not
On her own
She has His orders
To abide.

Do not be afraid
Death is all warm
Soft and kind …
To all those

Who trust
His Judgement.

*Gitanjali Badruddin*


## 135.  JESUS DIES ON THE CROSS

*He dispossessed himself, and took the nature of a slave, fashioned in
the likeness of men, and presenting himself to us in human form; and then
he lowered his own dignity, accepted an obedience which brought him to
death, death on a cross.* (Phil. 2,7-8; Knox)

*We too must be ready to lay down our lives for the sake of our brethren.*
(I John 3,16; Knox)


A few hours more,
A few minutes more,
A few instants more.
For thirty-three years it has been going on.
For thirty-three years you have lived fully
minute after minute.
You can no longer escape, now; you are there, at the
end of your life, at the end of  your road.
You are at the last extremity, at the edge of  a precipice.
You must take the last step,
The last step of love,
The last step of life that ends in death.
You hesitate.
Three hours are long, three hours of agony;
Longer than three years of life ,
Longer than thirty years of life.

You must decide, Lord, all is ready around you.
You are there, motionless, on your Cross.
You have renounced all activity other than  embracing
        these crossed planks for which you were made.
And yet, there is still life in your nailed body.
Let mortal flesh die, and make way for eternity.
Now, life slips from each limb, one by one, finding
                        refuge in his still beating heart

Immeasurable heart,
Overflowing heart,
Heart heavy as the world, the world of sins and miseries
                        that it bears.

Lord, one more effort.
Mankind is there, waiting unknowingly for the cry of
                        its  Saviour.

Your brothers are there; they need you.
Your Father bends over you, already holding out his
                        arms.
Lord, save us,
Save us.

See.
He has taken his heavy heart,
And,
Slowly,
Laboriously,
Alone between heaven and earth,
In the awesome night,

With passionate love,
He has gathered his life,
He has gathered the sin of the world,
And in a cry,
He has given *all*.
"Father, into thy hands I commit my spirit."

Christ has just died for us.

Lord, help me to die for you.
Help me to die for them.

Michel Quoist

Translated by Anne Marie De Commaile<br>and Agnes Mitchell Forsyth

## 136.   PRESUMPTION

Meeting with my Master on the road,
I put my sorrow to him,
And told him of my loss.
But as I spoke, my voice seemed over-loud,
And my fixed gaze pierced through him
To see a skeleton upon a Cross.

I must have been a drunkard upon grief
Thus to annihilate
Another's flesh and blood,
Making a fantasy for my relief
Equal to his fate
For fear that I should not be understood.

He took my proud reduction, and became
Instantly to my touch
Human, as a brother.
Mortal despair dissolved into a name,
And what I'd lost was such
As he and I could share with one another.

Richard Church


## 137.  YOU TAUGHT ME —

You taught me Waiting with Myself —
Appointment strictly kept —
You taught me fortitude of Fate —
This — also — I have learnt —
An Altitude of Death, that could
No bitterer debar
Than Life — had done — before it —
Yet — there is a Science more —

The Heaven you know — to understand
That you be not ashamed
Of Me — in Christ's bright Audience —
Upon the further Hand —

Emily Dickinson


## 138.  I MAY REAP

I who have not sown,

I too
By God's grace may come  to harvest
And proud,
As the bowed
Reapers
At the Assumption
Murmur thanksgiving.

*Patric   Kavanagh*


## 139. GOD'S TIME MUST END OUR TROUBLE

God doth not promise here to man, that He
Will free him quickly from his miserie;
But in His own time, and when He thinks fit,
Then He will give a happy end to it.

*Robert Herrick*


## 140.  VIVAMUS

When thou didst give thy love to me,
  Asking no more of gods or men
I vow'd I would contented be,
  If Fate should grant us summers ten.

But now that twice the term is sped,
  And ever young my heart and gay,
I fear the words that then I said,
  And turn my face from Fate away.

To bid thee happily good-bye
  I have no hope that I can see,
No way that I shall bravely die,
  Unless I give my life for thee.

*Robert Bridges*

## 141. NO MOURNING, BY REQUEST

Come not to mourn for me with solemn tread
Clad in dull weeds of sad and sable hue,
Nor weep because my tale of life's told through.
Casting light dust on my untroubled head.

Nor linger near me while the sexton fills
My grave with earth — but go gay-garlanded,
And in your halls a shining banquet spread
And gild your chambers o'er with daffodils.

Fill your tall goblets with white wine and red,
And sing brave songs of gallant love and true,
Wearing soft robes of emerald and blue,
And dance, as I your dances oft have led,
And laugh, as I have often laughed with you —
And be most merry — after I am dead.

*Winifred Holtby*

## 142.  POT-BOUND

O I am root-bound! In this earthen Pot
How many a strangling noose and writhing knot
Describe contorted misery! a tomb
Where one woe for another leaves not room!
A charnel-house of starved desires, whence all
Is gone of Humus and good Mineral,
Or anything on which a Plant might feed
Till it could blossom and produce a seed;
Where wretched Worms, to their own hurt,  have got
In by mischance, and poison all the pot:
Where the poor roots, for want of object fit,
Embrace the Drainage-crock, make much of it,
And glide, and feel, and search all ways in vain,
Sick for the Food and Space they can't  attain,
And to the pining Branches only send
A negative, a warning of the End;
For if a growing Plant's not potted-on,
Betimes, and given new soil, its hope is gone.

O Gardener (if Gardener there be)
Behold this yellow leaf, and succour me!
From wizened stem and flowerless twig infer
The panic of the roots, whose silent stir
If rendered vocal, would affront the sky
With a great Mob's most hoarse and dreadful cry!
Otap me out! The tangled mass uncoil,
And rid my root of the exhausted soil!
Prod, O prod forth the unlucky Worms, and send
 Them where they serve a salutary end;

The close-invested Drainage-crock pluck out,
Which the starved filaments have meshed about;
Spread out their aching toils, and then, O then,
Enlarge me into a clean Number Ten,
With some sweet rotted Turf, some crumbling Loam,
That I may feel myself at last at home,
And bud, and flourish, finally to be
A credit to my kind, and unto thee!

A long-retarded Plant, when thus relieved,
May grow so swiftly, and so thickly leaved
And richly budded, that its bright Ascent
And Blossoming are an Astonishment:
O give me leave thus to aspire and blow,
And come at last to the great Flower-show,
Where every past Despair and bygone Grief
I'll sublimate in each transcendent Leaf;
The bitter darkness of that former gloom
Will write in all the brilliance of a Bloom;
The absence of the Worm will celebrate
In Perfume worthy of an Emperor's state;
That all may say, "Why, here's a Flower indeed!"
And crave a Slip of me, or else a Seed.

Ruth Pitter

## 143. *From* **BRIC A BRAC**

What is to come we know not. But we know

That what has been was good — was good to show,
Better to hide and best of all to bear.
We are the masters of the days that were:
We have lived,we have loved,we have suffered...
even so.
Shall we not take the ebb who had the flow?
Life was our friend. Now, if it be our foe —
Dear, though it spoil and break us! —need we care
What is to come?

*W. E. Henley*

## 144.  CROSSING THE BAR

Sunset and evening star,
   And one clear call for me!
And may there be no moaning of the bar,
   When I put out to sea,

But such a tide as moving seems asleep
   Too full for sound and foam,
When that which drew from out the boundless deep
   Turns again home.

Twilight and evening bell,
   And after that the dark!
And may there be no sadness of farewell,
   When I embark;

For tho' from out our bourne of Time and Place
        The flood may bear me far
I hope to see my Pilot face to face
        When I have crost the bar.

*Alfred, Lord Tennyson*

# PART FOUR

# ALL SHALL BE WELL

## 145.  TEARES

God from our eyes all teares hereafter wipes,
And gives His Children kisses then, not stripes.

*Robert Herrick*


## 146  CLOSE, MORTAL EYES

Close, mortal eyes: open, my eyes in heaven.
On consolations that the poor devise,
On the clay image and the candles seven
    Close, mortal eyes.

Open upon the plains of the merry land,
Eternal eyes, on joy for ever whole:
Return with tidings I shall understand
    Eyes of may soul.

The soul has eyes: alas, she has no tongue,
She has no word of all the mysteries,
No syllable that may be said or sung.
    Close, mortal eyes.

*Ruth Pitter*

# 147. SHADOW

Even the beauty of the rose doth cast,
When its bright, fervid noon is past,
A still and lengthening shadow in the dust
    Till darkness come
    And take its strange dream home.

The transient bubbles of the water paint
'Neath their frail arch a shadow faint;
The golden nimbus of the windowed saint,
    Till shine the stars,
    Casts pale and trembling bars.

The loveliest thing earth hath, a shadow hath,
A dark and livelong hint of death,
Haunting it ever till its last faint  breath...
    Who, then, may tell
    The beauty of heaven's shadowless asphodel?

*Walter de la Mare*


# 148.  WHAT IS LIFE?

And what is Life? an hour-glass on the run
A mist retreating from the morning sun
    A busy bustling still repeated dream
Its length? A moment's pause, a moment's thought

And happiness A bubble on the stream
That in the act of siezing shrinks to nought

Vain hopes — what are they? Puffing gales of morn
That of its charms divests the dewy lawn
    And robs each flowret of its gem and dies
A cobweb hiding disappointments thorn
    Which stings more keenly thro' the thin disguise

And thou, 0 trouble? Nothing can suppose,
And sure the Power of Wisdom only knows,
    What need requireth thee.
So free and lib'ral as thy bounty flows,
    Some necessary cause must surely be.

And what is death? Is still the cause  unfound
The dark mysterious name of horrid sound
    A long and ling'ring sleep the weary crave —
And peace — where can its happiness abound?
    No where at all but Heaven and the grave

Then what is Life? When stript of its disguise
    A thing to be desir'd it cannot be
Since every thing that meets our foolish eyes
    Gives proof sufficient of its vanity
'Tis but a trial all must undergo
    To teach unthankful mortals how to prize
That happiness vain man's denied to know
    Untill he's call'd to claim it inthe skies.

*John Clare*

## 149.  LIFE AND DEATH

Frail Life! in which, through mists of human breath
We grope for truth, and make our progress slow,
Because by passion blinded; till, by death
Our passions ending, we begin to know.

O reverend Death! whose looks can soon advise
E'en scornful youth, while priests their doctrine waste;
Yet mocks us too; for he does make us wise,
When by his coming our affairs are past.

O harmless Death! whom still the valiant brave,
The wise expect, the sorrowful invite,
And all the good embrace, who know the grave
A short dark passage to eternal light.

*Sir William Davenant*


## 150. SONG OF PAIN

Out of my sorrow have I made these songs,
    Out of my sorrow;
Though somewhat of the making's eager pain
    From joy did borrow.

Some day, I trust God's purpose of Pain for me
    Shall be complete,

And then — to enter in the House of Joy…
    Prepare, my feet.

*Ivor Gurney*


## 151.  THE HOUR OF DEATH

*"Il est dans la nature d'aimer à se livrer à
l'idée même qu'on redoute."* — Corinne.


   Leaves have their time to fall,
And flowers to wither at the north wind's  breath,
   And stars to set — but all,
Thou hast *all* seasons for thine own, O Death!

   Day is for mortal care,
Eve, for glad meetings round the joyous  hearth,
   Night, for the dreams of sleep, the voice
                     of prayer —
But all for thee, thou mightiest of the earth.

   The banquet hath its hour —
Its feverish hour, of mirth, and song, and wine;
   There comes a day for grief's  o'erwhelming power,
A time for softer tears — but all are thine.

   Youth and the opening rose
May look like things too glorious for decay,
   And smile at thee — but thou art not of those
That wait the ripen'd bloom to seize their prey.
   Leaves have their time to fall,

And flowers to wither at the north wind's breath,
　　And stars to set — but all,
Thou hast *all* seasons for thine own, O Death!

　　We know when moons shall wane,
When summer birds from far shall　cross the sea,
　　When autumn's hue shall tinge the golden grain —
But who shall teach us when to look for thee!

　　Is it when spring's first gale
Comes forth to whisper where the violets lie?
　　Is it when roses in our paths grow pale? —
They have *one* season — *all* are ours to die!

　　Thou art where billows foam,
Thou art where music melts upon the air;
　　Thou art around us in our peaceful home,
And the world calls us forth — and thou art there.

　　Thou art where friend meets friend,
Beneath the shadow of the elm to rest —
　　Thou art where foe meets foe, and trumpets rend
The skies, and swords beat down the princely crest.

　　Leaves have their time to fall,
And flowers to wither at the north wind's　breath,
　　And stars to set — but all —
Thou hast *all* seasons for thine own, O Death!

*Felicia Hemans*

## 152.  UNTO EACH MAN —

Unto each man his handiwork, unto each  his crown,
    The just Fate gives;
Whoso takes the world's life on him and his  own
                                     lays down,
    He, dying so, lives.

Whoso bears the whole heaviness of the wronged
                                 world's weight
    And puts it by,
It is well with him suffering, though he face man's fate;
    How should he die?

Seeing death has no part in him any more, no power
    Upon his head;
He has bought this eternity with a little hour,
    And is not dead.

For an hour, if ye look for him, he is no more found,
    For one hour's space;
Then ye lift up your eyes to him and behold him
                                crowned,
    A deathless face.

On the mountains of memory, by the world's
                               well-springs,
    In all men's eyes,
Where the light of the life of him is on all past things,
    Death only dies,

Not the light that was quenched for us, nor the deeds
that were,
    Nor the ancient days,
Nor the sorrows not sorrowful, nor the face most fair
    Of perfect praise.

A. C. Swinburne

## 153.  COURAGE

O heart, hold thee secure
In this blind hour of stress,
Live on, love on, endure,
Uncowed, though comfortless.

Life's still the wondrous thing
It seemed in bygone peace,
Though woe now jar the string,
And all its music cease.

Even if thine own self have
No haven for defence;
Stand not the unshaken brave
To give thee confidence?

Worse than all worst 'twould be,
If thou, who art thine all,
Shatter ev'n their reality
    In thy poor fall!

Walter de la Mare

# 154.  "CRY WOE, WOE —"

O well for him who lives at ease
    With garnered gold in wide domain,
    Nor heeds the splashing of the rain,
The crashing down of forest trees.

O well for him who ne'er hath known
    The travail of the hungry years,
    A father grey with grief and tears,
A mother weeping all alone.

But well for him whose foot hath trod
    The weary road of toil and strife,
    Yet from the sorrows of his life
Builds ladders to be nearer God.

*Oscar Wilde*


# 155.  THE SILENT VOICES

When the dumb Hour, clothed in black,
Brings the Dreams about my bed,
Call me not so often back,
Silent Voices of the dead,
Toward the lowland ways behind me,
And the sunlight that is gone!
Call me rather, silent voices,
Forward to the starry track

Glimmering up the heights beyond me,
On, and always on!

*Alfred, Lord Tennyson*


## 156.  THE LAST INVOCATION

At the last, tenderly,
From the walls of the powerful fortress'd house,
From the clasp of the knitted locks, from the keep of
                                 the well-closed doors,
Let me be wafted.

Let me glide noiselessly forth;
With the key of softness unlock the locks —with
                                       a whisper,
Set ope the doors O soul.

Tenderly — be not impatient,
(Strong is your hold O mortal flesh,
Strong is your hold O love.)

*Walt Whitman*


## 157.   FATHER, TO THEE WE LOOK —
*Heaviness may endure for a night, but joy cometh in the morning*
Psalm xxx 5

Father, to Thee we look in all our sorrow.
Thou art the fountain whence our healing flows;

Dark though the night, joy cometh with the morrow;
Safely they rest who on Thy love repose.

When fond hopes fail and skies are dark before us,
When the vain cares that vex our life increase,
Comes with its calm the thought that Thou art o'er us,
And we grow quiet, folded in Thy peace.

Nought can affright us, on Thy goodness leaning;
Low in the heart faith singeth still her song;
Chastened by pain we learn life's deeper meaning,
And in our weakness Thou dost make us strong.

Patient, O heart, though heavy be thy sorrows;
Be not cast down, disquieted in vain;
Yet shalt thou praise Him, when these darkened
                                        furrows,
Where now He plougheth, wave with golden grain.

*F. L. Hosmer*


## 158.  DEATH

Though since thy first sad entrance by
                Just *Abels* blood,
'Tis now six thousand years well nigh,
And still thy sov'rainty holds good:
Yet by none art thou understood.

We talk and name thee with much ease
                As a tryed thing,

And every one can slight his lease
As if it ended in a Spring,
Which shades & bowers doth rent-free bring.

To thy dark land these heedless go:
           But there was *One*,
Who search'd it quite through to and fro,
And then returning, like the Sun,
Discover'd all, that there is done.

And since his death, we throughly see
           All thy dark way;
Thy shades but thin and narrow be,
Which his first looks will quickly fray:
Mists make but triumphs for the day.

As harmless violets, which give
           Their virtues here
For salves and syrups, while they live,
Do after calmly disappear,
And neither grieve, repine, nor fear:

So dye his servants; and as sure
           Shall they revive.
Then let not dust your eyes obscure,
But lift them up, where still alive,
Though fled from you, their spirits hive.

*Henry Vaughan*

# 159. THE INCARNATION, AND PASSION

Lord! when thou didst thy selfe undresse
Laying by thy robes of glory,
To make us more, thou wouldst be lesse,
And becam'st a wofull story.

To put on Clouds instead of light,
And cloath the morning-starre with dust,
Was a translation of such height
As, but in thee, was ne'r exprest;

Brave wormes, and Earth! that thus could have
A God Enclos'd within your Cell,
Your maker pent up in a grave,
Life lockt in death, heav'n in a shell;

Ah, my deare Lord! what couldst thou spye
In this impure, rebellious clay,
That made thee thus resolve to dye
For those that kill thee every day?

O what strange wonders could thee move
To slight thy precious bloud, and breath!
Sure it was *Love*, my Lord; for *Love*
Is only stronger far than death.

*Henry Vaughan*

# 160. FOR CORDER CATCHPOOL

"Death is no enemy to those who seek
And scale the mountain-tops of life and time,
To meet their end upon some mighty peak
Of man's experience, ruthless and sublime.
Yet not their end; for who that sees this place
Can doubt the Maker's pattern, shade and sun,
Defeat redeemed by victory, triumphs won
Which light the blazing glory of His Face?

"And how should we forget thee, undismayed
By years or peril, whose untarnished soul
Soared free to find its own allotted goal;
Leaving the mortal man, his ransom paid,
To sleep serene amid the snows untrod
where dwells the awful Majesty of God."

*Vera Brittain*

# 161.   HOLY SONNET X

Death be not proud, though some have called thee
Mighty and dreadful, for, thou art not soe,
For, those, whom thou think'st, thou dost overthrow,
Die not, poore death, nor yet canst thou kill mee.
From rest and sleepe, which but thy pictures bee,
Much pleasure, then from thee, much more must flow,
And soonest our best men with thee doe goe,
Rest of their bones, and soules deliverie.

Thou art slave to Fate, Chance, kings, and
desperate men,
And dost with poyson, warre, and sicknesse dwell,
And poppie, or charmes can make us sleepe  as well,
And better than thy stroake; why swell'st thou then?
One short sleepe past, wee wake eternally,
And death shall be no more; death, thou shalt die.

*John Donne*


## 162. DEATH

Death, thou wast once an uncouth hideous thing,
Nothing but bones,
The sad effect of sadder grones:
Thy mouth was open, but thou couldst not sing.

For we consider'd thee as at some six
Or ten yeares hence,
After the losse of life and sense,
Flesh being turn'd to dust, and bones to sticks.

We lookt on this side of thee, shooting short;
Where we did finde
The shells of fledge souls left behinde,
Dry dust, which sheds no tears, but may extort.

But since our Saviours death did put some bloud
Into thy face;
Thou art grown fair and full of grace,
Much in request, much sought for as a good.

For we do now behold thee gay and glad,
                As at dooms-day;
When souls shall wear their new aray,
And all thy bones with beautie shall be clad.

Therefore we can go die as sleep, and trust
                Half that we have
            Unto an honest faithfull grave;

Making our pillows either down, or dust.

George Herbert

## 163. AND DEATH SHALL HAVE NO DOMINION

And death shall have no dominion.
Dead men naked they shall be one
With the man in the wind and the west moon;
When their bones are picked clean and the  clean bones
                                        gone,
They shall have stars at elbow and foot;
Though they go mad they shall be sane,
Though they sink through the sea they shall rise again;
Though lovers be lost love shall not;
And death shall have no dominion.

And death shall have no dominion.
Under the windings of the sea
They lying long shall not die windily;
Twisting on racks when sinews give way,
Strapped to a wheel, yet they shall not break;

Faith in their hands shall snap in two,
And the unicorn evils run them through;
Split all ends up they shan't crack;
And death shall have no dominion.

And death shall have no dominion.
No more may gulls cry at their ears
Or waves break loud on the seashores;
Where blew a flower may a flower no more
Lift its head to the blows of the rain;
Though they be mad and dead as nails,
Heads of the characters hammer through daisies;
Break in the sun till the sun breaks down,
And death shall have no dominion.

*Dylan Thomas*


## 164. LIGHT SHINING OUT OF DARKNESS

God moves in a mysterious way,
    His wonders to perform;
He plants his footsteps in the sea,
    And rides upon the storm.

Deep in unfathomable mines
    Of never failing skill,
He treasures up his bright designs,
    And works his sovereign will.

Ye fearful saints, fresh courage take,
    The clouds ye so much dread

Are big with mercy, and shall break
   In blessings on your head.

Judge not the Lord by feeble sense,
   But trust him for his grace;
Behind a frowning providence,
   He hides a smiling face.

His purposes will ripen fast,
   Unfolding ev'ry hour;
The bud may have a bitter taste,
   But sweet will be the flow'r.

Blind unbelief is sure to err,
   And scan his work In vain;
God is his own interpreter,
   And he will make it plain.

*William Cowper*

## 165.  ODE TO DEATH

Come, lovely and soothing death,
Undulate round the world, serenely arriving, arriving,
In the day, in the night, to all, to each,
Sooner or later delicate death.

Prais'd be the fathomless universe,
For life and joy, and for objects and knowledge curious.
And for love, since love — but praise! praise! praise!
For the sure-enwinding arms of cool-enfolding death.

Dark mother always gliding near with soft feet,
Have none chanted for thee a chant of fullest welcome?
Then I chant it for thee, I glorify thee above all.
I bring thee a song that when thou must indeed come,
come unfalteringly.

Approach strong deliveress,
When it is so, when thou has taken them I joyously sing
the dead,
Lost in the loving floating ocean of thee,
Laved in the flood of thy bliss, O Death.

From me to thee glad serenades,
Dances for thee I propose saluting thee, adornments
and feastings for thee,
And the sights of the open landscape and the
high-spread sky are fitting,
And life and the fields, and the huge and thoughtful
night.

The night in silence under many a star,
The ocean shore and the husky whispering wave
whose voice I know,
And the soul turning to thee O vast and
well-veil'd death,
And the body gratefully nestling close to thee.

Over the tree tops I float thee a song,

Over the rising and sinking waves, over the myriad
fields and the prairies wide,

Over the dense-pack'd cities all and teeming wharves
                                    and ways,
I float this carol with joy, with joy to thee,  O  death.

*Walt Whitman*


## 166.  DEATH

Death, that struck when I was most confiding
In my certain Faith of Joy to be,
Strike again, Time's withered branch dividing
From the fresh root of Eternity!

Leaves, upon Time's branch, were growing brightly
Full of sap and full of silver dew;
Birds, beneath its shelter, gathered nightly;
Daily, round its flowers, the wild birds flew.

Sorrow passed and plucked the golden blossom,
Guilt stripped off the foliage in its pride;
But within its parent's kindly bosom
Flowed for ever Life's restoring tide.

Little mourned I for the parted Gladness,
For the vacant nest and silent song;
Hope was there and laughed me out of sadness,
Whispering, "Winter will not linger long."

And behold, with tenfold increase blessing
Spring adorned the beauty-burdened spray;
Wind and rain and fervent heat caressing

Lavished glory on its second May.

High it rose; no winged grief could sweep it;
Sin was scared to distance with its shine:
Love and its own life had power to keep it
From all wrong, from every blight but thine!

Heartless Death, the young leaves droop and languish!
Evening's gentle air may still restore —
No, the morning sunshine mocks my anguish —
Time for me must never blossom more!

Strike it down — that other boughs may flourish
Where that perished sapling used to be;
Thus, at least, its mouldering corpse will nourish
 That from which it sprung — Eternity.

Emily Brontë


## 167.  WORDS ARE A DYING SUN

Words are a sun
               finally
               sinking
                    behind the rim of silence;
words
    are
      a dying sun.

Our cold twilight words
                    before darkness and silence

are slow words
               that sing in the evening of man.

Who can give words of love
                              to the aged
                              and tired
                              and hoar-headed;
who will love man,
     man empty and decaying and near blind
     man who hides the ugly death signs
     with senile dreams
                         of long-ago youth
                         and beauty
                         and innocence.

The sun of righteousness,
     the Word of truth,
       will give words of love to man,
     will rise in the vision of those
whose eyes he has opened in fear.
                         opened to the coming silent death
                              that
                 is
              dark
dark,
     death darker than a cold
                         sunless solar system

The sun of righteousness,
     the sun of righteousness
          the sun of righteousness
shall arise with healing in his wings,

Then only will the earth have its rest,
        its peace;
            its fulfilment;
                its meaning;
then only will it break into cries of joy.


        But those that see him will be few:
they will first tread
the sinking and setting of the sun
before its time of death;
            they alone will therefore dance the new arising
for they alone will see
                their sickness and their
                    age and their decay
and they alone will first have early been caught
            in their lonely vision
by
    the dying
                of the old tired sun.


Words
        are
            a dying sun,
and words of love give long shadows.

*Colin Duriez*


## 168.  FIVE SONNETS

1.
You think that we who do not shout and shake

Our fists at God when youth or bravery die
Have colder blood or hearts less apt to ache
Than yours who rail. I know you do. Yet why?
You have what sorrow always longs to find,
Someone to blame, some enemy in chief;
Anger's the anaesthetic of the mind,
It does men good, it fumes away their grief.
We feel the stroke like you; so far our fate
Is equal. After that, for us begin
Half-hopeless labours, learning not to hate,
And then to want, and then (perhaps) to win
A high, unearthly comfort, angel's food,
That seems at first mockery to flesh and blood.

2.

There's a repose, a safety (even a taste
Of something like revenge?) in fixed despair
Which we're forbidden. We have to rise with haste
And start to climb what seems a crazy stair.
Our consolation (for we are consoled,
So much of us, I mean, as may be left
After the dreadful process has unrolled)
For one bereavement makes us more bereft.
It asks for all we have, to the last shred;
Read Dante, who had known its best and worst —
He was bereaved and he was comforted
—No one denies it, comforted — but first
Down to the frozen centre, up the vast
Mountain of pain, from world to world, he passed.

3.

Of this we're certain; no one who dared knock

At heaven's door for earthly comfort found
Even a door — only smooth, endless rock,
And save the echo of his cry no sound.
It's dangerous to listen; you'll begin
To fancy that those echoes (hope can play
Pitiful tricks) are answers from within;
Far better to turn, grimly sane, away.
Heaven cannot thus, Earth cannot ever, give
The thing we want. We ask what isn't there
And by our asking water and make live
That very part of love which must despair
And die and go down cold into the earth
Before there's talk of springtime and rebirth.

4.

Pitch your demands heaven-high and they'll be met.
Ask for the Morning Star and take (thrown in)
Your earthly love. Why, yes; but how to set
One's foot on the first rung, how to begin?
The silence of one voice upon our ears
Beats like the waves; the coloured morning seems
A lying brag; the face we loved appears
Fainter each night, or ghastlier, in our dreams.
"That long way round which Dante trod was meant
For mighty saints and mystics not for me,"
So Nature cries. Yet if we once assent
To Nature's voice, we shall be like the bee
That booms against the window-pane for hours
Thinking that way to reach the laden flowers.

5.

"If we could speak to her," my doctor said,

"And told her, 'Not that way All, all in vain
You weary out your wings and bruise your head,'
Might she not answer, buzzing at the pane,
'Let queens and mystics and religious bees
Talk of such inconceivables as glass;
The blunt lay worker flies at what she sees,
Look there — ahead, ahead — the flowers, the grass!'
We catch her in a handkerchief (who knows
What rage she feels, what terror, what despair?)
And shake her out — and gaily out she goes
Where quivering flowers stand thick in summer air,
To drink their hearts. But left to her own will
She would have died upon the window-sill."

C. S.  Lewis


## 169.  NO COWARD SOUL...

No coward soul is mine,
No trembler in the world's storm-troubled sphere!
I see Heaven's glories shine,
And Faith shines equal, arming me from Fear

O God within my breast,
Almighty ever-present Deity!

Life, that in me hast rest,
As I, Undying Life, have power in thee!

Vain are the thousand creeds
That move men's hearts, unutterably vain;

Worthless as withered weeds,
Or idlest froth amid the boundless main,

To waken doubt in one
Holding so last by thy infinity,
So surely anchored on
The steadfast rock of Immortality.

With wide-embracing love
Thy spirit animates eternal years,
Pervades and broods above,
Changes, sustains, dissolves, creates, and rears.

Though earth and moon were gone,
And suns and universes ceased to be,
And thou wert left alone,
Every Existence would exist in thee.

There is not room for Death
Nor atom that his might could render void;
Since thou art Being and Breath
And what thou art may never be destroyed.

Emily Brontë

## 170. *From* LITTLE GIDDING

IV.

The dove descending breaks the air
With flame of incandescent terror

Of which the tongues declare
The one discharge from sin and error.
The only hope, or else despair
    Lies in the choice of pyre or pyre—
    To be redeemed from fire by fire.

Who then devised the torment? Love.
Love is the unfamiliar Name
Behind the hands that wove
The intolerable shirt of flame
Which human power cannot remove.
    We only live, only suspire
    Consumed by either fire or fire.

V.

What we call the beginning is often the end
And to make an end is to make a beginning.
The end is where we start from. And every phrase
And sentence that is right (where every word is at home,
Taking its place to support the others,
The word neither diffident nor ostentatious,
An easy commerce of the old and the new,
The common word exact without vulgarity,
The formal word precise but not pedantic,
The complete consort dancing together)
Every phrase and every sentence is an end and
                        a beginning,
Every poem an epitaph. And any action
Is a step to the block, to the fire, down the sea's throat
Or to an illegible stone: and that is where we start.
We die with the dying:
See, they depart, and we go with them.

We are born with the dead:
See, they return, and bring us with them.
The moment of the rose and the moment of
                              the  yew-tree
Are of equal duration. A people without  history
Is not redeemed from time, for history is a pattern
Of timeless moments. So, while the light fails
On a winter's afternoon, in a secluded chapel
History is now and England.

With the drawing of this Love and the voice of
                              this Calling

We shall not cease from exploration
And the end of all our exploring
Will be to arrive where we started
And know the place for the first time.
Through the unknown, remembered gate
When the last of earth left to discover
Is that which was the beginning;
At the source of the longest river
The voice of the hidden waterfall
And the children in the apple-tree
Not known, because not looked for
But heard, half-heard, in the stillness
Between two waves of the sea.
Quick now, here, now, always—
A condition of complete simplicity
(Costing not less than everything)
And all shall be well and
All manner of thing shall be well
When the tongues of flame are in-folded

Into the crowned knot of fire
And the fire and the rose are one.

*T. S. Eliot*

## 173.  ST. JOHN'S GOSPEL 14:1-6

1.  Let not your heart be troubled: ye believe in God, believe also in me.
2.  In my Father's house are many mansions: if *it were not so*, I would have told you. I go to prepare a place for you.
3.  And if I go and prepare a place for you, I will come again and receive you unto myself; that where I am, *there* ye may be also.
4.  And whither I go ye know, and the way ye know.
5.  Thomas saith unto him, Lord, we know not whither thou goest; and how can we know the way?
6.  Jesus saith unto him. I am the way, the truth, and the life: no man cometh unto the Father, but by me.

## 172.  NATURE.

As a fond mother, when the day is o'er,
　Leads by the hand her little child to bed,

Half willing, half reluctant to be led,
And leave his broken playthings on the floor,
Still gazing at them through the open door,
   Nor wholly reassured and comforted
   By promises of others in their stead,
   Which, though more splendid, may not please
                                     him more;
So Nature deals with us, and takes away
   Our playthings one by one, and by the hand
   Leads us to rest so gently, that we go
Scarce knowing if we wished to go or stay,
   Being too full of sleep to understand
   How far the unknown transcends, the what
                                     we know.

*Henry  W. Longfellow*


## 173.  FAR AWAY IS THE LAND...

Far away is the land of rest;
Thousand miles are stretched between,
Many a mountain's stormy crest,
Many a desert void of green.

Wasted, worn is the traveller,
Dark his heart and dim his eye;
Without hope or comforter,
Faltering, faint, and ready to die.

Often he looks to the ruthless sky,
Often he looks o'er his dreary road;

Often he wishes down to lie
And render up life's tiresome load.

But yet faint not, mournful man;
Leagues on leagues are left behind
Since your sunless course began;
Then go on to toil resigned.

If you still despair control,
Hush its whispers in your breast;
You shall reach the final goal,
You shall win the land of rest.

Emily Brontë

## 176.  PILGRIM'S SONG

Who would True valour see,
Let him come hither;
One here will constant be,
Come Wind, come Weather.
There's no Discouragement
Shall make him once relent

His first avow'd intent
To be a Pilgrim.
Who so beset him round
With dismal Stories
Do but themselves confound,
His Strength the more is;

No Lion can him fright.
He'll with a Giant fight,
But he will have a right
To be a Pilgrim.
    Hobgoblin nor foul Fiend
Can daunt his spirit;
He knows he at the end
Shall Life inherit.
Then Fancies fly away.
He'll fear not what men say,
He'll labour night and day
To be a Pilgrim.

*John Bunyan*


## 175.   GODS BOUNTY

God, as He's potent, so He's likewise known,
To give us more then Hope can fix upon.


## FREE WELCOME

God He refuseth no man; but makes way
For All that now come, or hereafter may.

*Robert Herrick*

# 176.   THE 23RD PSALME

The God of love my shepherd is,
    And he that doth me feed:
While he is mine, and I am his,
    What can I want or need?

He leads me to the tender grasse,
    Where I both feed and rest;
Then to the streams that gently passe:
    In both I have the best.

Or if I stray, he doth convert
    And bring my minde in frame:
And all this not for my desert,
    But for his holy name.

Yea, in deaths shadie black abode
    Well may I walk, not fear:
For thou art with me; and thy rod
    To guide, thy staff to bear.

Nay, thou dost make me sit and dine,
    Even in my enemies sight:
My head with oyl, my cup with wine
    Runnes over day and night.

Surely thy sweet and wondrous love
    Shall measure all my dayes;

And as it never shall remove,
    So neither shall my praise.

George Herbert

## 177.  THE FEAST

O come away,
Make no delay,
    Come while my heart is clean & steddy!
While Faith and Grace
Adorn the place,
    Making dust and ashes ready.

No bliss here lent
Is permanent,
    Such triumphs poor flesh cannot merit;
Short sips and sights
Endear delights,
    Who seeks for more, he would inherit.

Come then true bread,
Quickning the dead,
    Whose eater shall not, cannot dye,
Come, antedate
On me that state
    Which brings poor dust the victory.

Henry Vaughan

# 178.  DEATHBED

Now, when the frail and fine-spun
Web of mortality
Gapes, and lets slip
What we have loved so long
From out our lighted present
Into the trackless dark

We turn, blinded,
Not to the Christ in Glory,
Stars about His feet,

But to the Son of Man,
Back from the tomb,
Who built fires, ate fish,
Spoke with friends, and walked
A dusty road at evening.

Here, in this room, in
This stark and timeless moment,
We hear those footsteps

And
With suddenly lifted hearts
Acknowledge
The irrelevance of death.

*Evangeline Paterson*

## 179.  SO HE PASSED OVER...

So he pass'd over, and all the trumpets
sounded for him on the other side.

*John Bunyan*

# INDEX OF AUTHORS

# ACKNOWLEDGEMENTS

Every effort has been made to trace copyright holders of poems in this anthology, and the editor would like to thank the authors (and their representatives or publishers) for their generosity in allowing the following works to be included in *And All Shall Be Well.*

Virago Ltd for *"Perhaps"* and *"For Corder Catchpool"* by Vera Brittain.

Laurence Pollinger Ltd and the Estate of Richard Church for *"The Presumption"* by Richard Church.

Harrap Ltd for *"Wayside Crucifix"* by Les Cotterell from *Poems from Italy.*

The Literary Trustees of Walter de la Mare and the Society of Authors as their representatives for *"Absence"*, *"Goodbye"*, *"Alone"*, *"Here Sleeps"* and *"Courage"* by Walter de la Mare.

Chatto and Windus Ltd and the author for *"A Dream"*, *"Elegy"* and *"At Sixty"* by Patric Dickinson.

Faber and Faber Ltd for *"Second Opinion"* by Douglas Dunn from *Elegies.*

Faber and Faber Ltd for an extract from *"Little Gidding"* by T. S. Eliot.

A. P. Watt Ltd. on behalf of the Executors of the Estate of Robert Graves for *"The Theme of Death"* by Robert Graves.

David Higham Associates Ltd. for *"Absence"* and *"A Requiem"* by Elizabeth Jennings.

Elizabeth Kavanagh for *"I May Reap"* and *"Mary"* by Patrick Kavanagh.

Randle Manwaring for his poems *"Dreams"*, *"Absence*

*and Return*", "*For Sale*" and "*Pine Forest*".

Faber and Faber Ltd. for "*The Absent*" by Edwin Muir from *The Collected Works of Edwin Muir*.

David Higham Associates Ltd for "*The Cock's Nest*" by Norman Nicholson from *A Local Habitation*.

Ruth Pitter for her poems "*A Natural Sorrow*", "*Joy and Grief*", "*The Bridge*", "*Close, Mortal Eyes*" and "*Pot Bound*".

Gill and Macmillan Ltd for "*Jesus Dies on the Cross*" by Michel Quoist, translated by Anne-Marie de Comaille and Agnes Mitchell Forsyth, from *Prayers of Life*.

Robson Books Ltd for "*Talking of Death*" and "*The Mourners*" by Vernon Scannell, from *New and Collected Poems, 1950-1980*.

Routledge and Kegan Paul for "*The Separation of Grief*" by Jon Silkin from *Psalm with Their Spoils*.

Macmillan London Ltd. for "*I Have Got My Leave*", "*On the Day When Death Will Know*" and "*Deliver Me from My Own Shadows*" by Rabindranath Tagore.

David Higham Associates Ltd for "*Death Shall Have No Dominion*" by Dylan Thomas, from *The Poems of Dylan Thomas* (Dent).

Penguin Books Ltd for "*Day by Day*" by Guiseppe Ungaretti, translated by Patrick Creagh, from *Selected Poems by Guiseppe Ungaretti* (Penguin Modern European Poets, 1971).

A.. P. Watt Ltd., on behalf of Michael B. Yeats and Macmillan London Ltd, for "*The Cloak, The Boat, and The Shoes*" by W. B. Yeats, from *The Collected Poems of W. B. Yeats*.

198

# ISIS

## large print and audio books

If you have enjoyed reading this book, you will be pleased to know that many more titles are available.

We have listed a selection on the next few pages. These are available as large print books or unabridged audio books; some are available in both book and audio tape form.

Please write to us at the address below if you require further information or contact your local librarian.

Any suggestions you may have for new large print or audio titles will be very welcome.

**ISIS, 55 St Thomas' Street, Oxford OX1 1JG, ENGLAND; tel. (0865) 250333**

# INSPIRATIONAL

| | |
|---|---|
| Rabbi Lionel Blue | **Kitchen Blues** |
| Victor Gollancz & Barbara Greene | **God of a Hundred Names** |
| Christopher Idle | **Famous Hymns and Their Stories** |
| Christopher Nolan | **Under the Eye of the Clock** |
| Beverley Parkin | **Say it With Flowers** |
| Beverley Parkin | **Flowers with Love** |
| Harry Secombe | **Highway** |
| | **Your Favourite Songs of Praise** |

# POETRY

| | |
|---|---|
| Lord Birkenhead (editor) | **John Betjeman's Early Poems** |
| Joan Duce | **I Remember, I Remember...** (Book and Audio) |
| Joan Duce | **Remember, If You Will...** |
| Robert Louis Stevenson | **A Child's Garden of Verses** |

# BIOGRAPHY AND AUTOBIOGRAPHY

| | |
|---|---|
| Bill Adler | **Fred Astaire** |
| Charles Allen | **Plain Tales from the Raj** |
| Chuck Ashman & Pamela Trescott | **Cary Grant** |
| Hilary Bailey | **Vera Brittain** |
| Ronnie Barker | **It's Hello From Him** |
| Trevor Barnes | **Terry Waite** |
| Winifred Beechey | **The Rich Mrs Robinson** |
| Christabel Beilenberg | **The Past is Myself** |
| Cilla Black | **Step Inside** |
| Sydney Biddle Barrows | **Mayflower Madam** |
| Piers Brendon | **Winston Churchill (Audio)** |
| Peter Harry Brown | **Such Devoted Sisters: Those Fabulous Gabors** |
| Michael Burn | **Mary and Richard** |
| Patrick Campbell | **Selections from 35 Years on the Job** |
| Winston S Churchill | **Memories and Adventures** |
| Joe Collins | **A Touch of Collins** |
| Bill Cosby | **Time Flies** |
| George Courtauld | **Odd Noises from the Barn** |
| Mary Craig | **The Crystal Spirit: Lech Walesa and his Poland** |
| Peter Cushing | **An Autobiography (Book and Audio)** |
| Peter Cushing | **'Past Forgetting'** |
| Roald Dahl | **Going Solo** |
| Betty Davis | **This 'n' That** |
| C Day Lewis | **Sagittarius Rising (Audio)** |
| David Duff | **George and Elizabeth (Audio)** |
| Jerry Epstein | **Remembering Charlie** |
| Peter Evans | **Ari: The Life and Times of Aristotle Socrates Onassis** |

# BIOGRAPHY AND AUTOBIOGRAPHY

| | |
|---|---|
| Diana Farr | **Five at 10: Prime Ministers' Consorts Since 1957** |
| David Fingleton | **Kiri** |
| Angela Fox | **Slightly Foxed** |
| Michael Freeland | **A Salute to Irving Berlin** |
| Joyce Fussey | **Cats in the Coffee** |
| Joyce Fussey | **Cows in the Corn** |
| Joyce Fussey | **'Milk My Ewes and Weep'** |
| Eve Garnett | **First Affections** |
| Ralph Glasser | **Growing Up in the Gorbals** (Audio) |
| Jon Godden & Rumer Godden | **Two under the Indian Sun** |
| Joyce Grenfell | **Darling Ma** |
| Unity Hall | **Philip** |
| Helen Hayes | **Loving Life** |
| Bob Hope | **Confessions of a Hooker** |
| Graham Jenkins | **Richard Burton, My Brother** |
| Penny Junor | **Charles** |
| Imran Kahn | **All Round View** |
| Roger Kahn | **Joe and Marilyn** |
| Julia Keay | **The Spy Who Never Was** |
| Laurie Lee | **As I Walked Out One Midsummer Morning** (Audio) |
| Laurie Lee | **Cider with Rosie** (Audio) |

# BIOGRAPHY AND AUTOBIOGRAPHY

| | |
|---|---|
| Laurie Lee | **I Can't Stay Long** (Audio) |
| Maureen Lipman | **How Was it for You?** |
| Vincent V Loomis | **Amelia Earhart** |
| Suzanne Lowry | **Cult of Diana** |
| Ralph G Martin | **Charles & Diana** |
| John McCabe | **Mr Laurel and Mr Hardy** |
| Jeanine McMullen | **Wind in the Ash Tree** |
| Peter Medawar | **Memoir of a Thinking Radish** |
| Spike Milligan | **Adolf Hitler: My Part in His Downfall** (Book and Audio) |
| Spike Milligan | **Mussolini: His Part in My Downfall** (Audio) |
| Spike Milligan | **Rommel? Gunner Who?** and **Monty: His Part in My Victory** (Audio) |
| Spike Milligan | **Where Have All the Bullets Gone?** (Audio) |
| Eugene McCarthy | **Up 'Til Now** |
| Ray Moore | **Tomorrow is Too Late** |
| Joe Morella & Edward Z Epstein | **Forever Lucy** |
| Joe Morella & Edward Z Epstein | **Loretta Young** |
| Eric Newby | **Love and War in the Apennines** (Book and Audio) |
| Eric Newby | **Something Wholesale** |
| Christopher Nolan | **Under the Eye of the Clock** (Book and Audio) |
| Barry Norman | **The Hollywood Greats** |

# BIOGRAPHY AND AUTOBIOGRAPHY

# SHORT STORIES AND ESSAYS

|  |  |
|---|---|
|  | **Echoes of Laughter** |
| Jorges Louis Borges | **The Book of Sand** |
| Angela Carter | **Fireworks** |
| Joseph Conrad | **The Heart of Darkness** (Audio) |
| A E Coppard | **Selected Stories** |
| Roald Dahl | **Roald Dahl's Book of Ghost Stories** |
| Roald Dahl | **Kiss Kiss** |
| M F K Fisher | **Sister Age** |
| E M Forster | **The New Collected Short Stories** (Audio) |
| Jane Gardam | **The Sidmouth Letters** |
| Leon Garfield | **Shakespeare Stories** |
| Mrs Gaskell | **Four Short Stories** |
| William Golding | **The Hot Gates** |
| Thomas Hardy | **Wessex Tales** |
| Duff Hart-Davis | **Country Matters** |
| Henry James | **Daisy Miller** |
| M R James | **A Warning to the Curious** (Book and Audio) |
| Bernard Levin | **The Way We Live Now** |
| Barry Pain | **The Eliza Stories** |
| Robert J Randisi (editor) | **An Eye for Justice** |
| Saki | **Beasts and Superbeasts** |
| E OE Somerville & Martin Ross | **Further Experiences of an Irish RM** |
| E OE Somerville & Martin Ross | **In Mr Knox's Country** |
| Edmund Wilson | **Memoirs of Hecate County** |
| Marguerite Yourcenar | **Oriental Tales** |

# POETRY AND DRAMA

# MEDICAL AND SELF HELP

|  |  |
|---|---|
|  | **Longman Medical Dictionary** |
| Christiaan Barnard | **Your Healthy Heart** |
| William H Bates | **Better Eyesight without Glasses** |
| Pat Blair | **Know Your Medicines** |
| Dr Robert Buckman | **I Don't Know What to Say** |
| Robert N Butler & Myrna I Butler | **Love and Sex After 40** |
| Margaret Ford | **'In Touch' at Home** |
| Margaret Hills | **Curing Arthritis** |
| Tony Lake | **Loneliness: Why it Happens and How To Overcome It** |
| Tony Lake | **Living with Grief** |
| Letts Retirement Guides | **Good Health** |
| Dr Patrick Mckeon | **Coping with Depression and Elation** |
| Dr Brice Pitt | **Making the Most of Middle Age** |
| Dr Tom Smith | **Living With High Blood Pressure** |
| Elaine Stritch | **Am I Blue? Living with Diabetes, and, Dammit, Having Fun** |
| George Target | **Your Arthritic Hip and You** |
| Dr Peter Tyrer | **How to Sleep Better** |
| Lynn Underwood | **One's Company** |
| Claire Weekes | **More Help for Your Nerves** |
| Betty Jane Wylie | **Beginnings** |
| Dr R M Youngson | **Stroke!** |

# ALSO AVAILABLE